Tour de ...

Raffi Youredjian

To my parents,
for whom I have yet to produce a grandchild

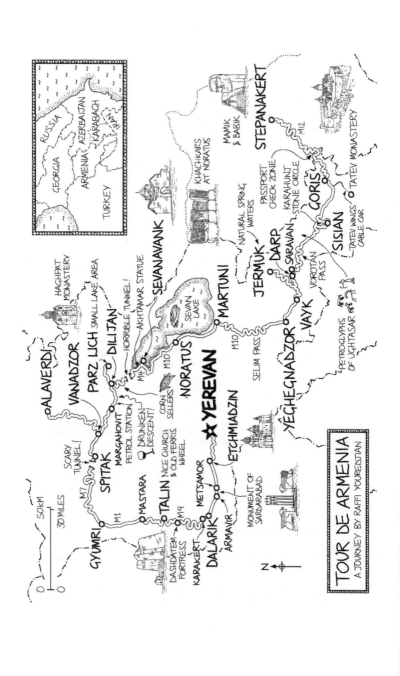

TOUR DE ARMENIA
A JOURNEY BY RAFFI YOURENTSIAN

RUSSIA
GEORGIA
ARMENIA
AZERBAIJAN
KARABACH
TURKEY
IRAN

50 KM
30 MILES

N

★ YEREVAN

GYUMRI
MASTARA
TALIN NICE CHURCH & OLD FERRIS WHEEL
KARAKERT
DASHDATEM FORTRESS
DALARIK
ARMAVIR
METSAMOR
MONUMENT OF SARNARABAD
ETCHMIADZIN
NORATUS
CORN SELLERS!
DRUNKEN DESCENT!
MARGAHOVIT PETROL STATION
SPITAK
SCARY TUNNEL!
VANADZOR
ALAVERDI
HAGHPAT MONASTERY
PARZ LICH SMALL LAKE AREA
DILIJAN
HORRIBLE TUNNEL!
AKHTAMAR STATUE
SEVANAVANK
SEVAN LAKE
KHACHKARS AT NORATUS
MARTUNI
YEGHEGNADZOR
SELIM PASS
JERMUK
DARP
SARAVAN
NATURAL SPRING WATERS
VAYK
VOROTAN PASS
PETROGLYPHS OF UGHTASAR
PASSPORT CHECK ZONE
KARAHUNT STONE CIRCLE
SISIAN
GORIS
STEPANAKERT
MAMIK & BABIK
TATEV MONASTERY
TATEV WINGS CABLE CAR

M7
M1
M9
M10
M11
M12

Chapter 1

This Is Going To Be The Trip

'What kind of girl should I marry, Grandma?'

'Oh, darling, just someone nice who will look after you and make you happy.'

'Can she be from Africa?'

My grandmother smiled sweetly. 'No, darling, it wouldn't work, it's too different.'

'Can she be Jewish, Grandma?'

Once again she smiled, but with a bit more sternness (recalling her childhood in Palestine, I assumed, and the 'relocation'). 'No, darling, it would be better if she wasn't Jewish.'

'How about British?'

'They're worse than men.'

'American?'

'They live in the clouds. Fantasyland.'

'How about an Armenian girl from America?' I asked.

'They're too spoiled, they'll milk all your money.' (She meant all the money she was going to leave us).

Finally I asked if she could be *Hayastantsi* (an Armenian from the Republic of Armenia).

'No!' she responded firmly. Her long-held theory was that they were all crooks.

If only she was still with us; I could ask about the suitability of a Chinese bride, or someone from the Kombai tribe in Papua New Guinea. Grandma was full of prejudices and she could hold a grudge for thirty years against a friend who wouldn't share a recipe, but she was still one of the greatest people I've known. For all eternity nobody would be good enough for her grandson.

But that didn't stop me looking.

* * *

Armenia is located where Europe meets Asia in the Southern Caucasus, bordering Turkey to the west, Iran to the south, Azerbaijan to the east and Georgia in the north. It's not the most prominent slab of land on a world map, being shaped like a miniature landlocked Italy without the boot. But it's got a rich heritage, one that can be traced back to very early civilizations. The history of its kingdoms is filled with beauty, religious devotion, brutality and sadness. Basically it's like a Leonard Cohen song.

Like most Armenians around the world, I wasn't born in Armenia, nor have I ever lived there. I made my first visit when I was nineteen and returned a couple of times to work as a volunteer teacher in some of the poorer villages. Although my stays there were very rewarding, I never felt like I really saw the country the way I wanted to. The traveller's instinct in me made me want to go out and explore, see more of this place I called my homeland, so I dreamt up my grand adventure, my Tour de Armenia. I bought some maps and loosely planned a 1,000-kilometre cycling trip starting in the west, in the capital city, Yerevan, and ending in the east, in Stepanakert, the capital of the war-ravaged region of Karabagh. The ride would be strenuous as the landscape is mountainous and the road full of high passes. I gave myself a month.

I am no stranger to long bike rides. I once rode on a 2,000-kilometre journey along Route 66, riding from

Chicago, through the heart of America as far as Amarillo, Texas. I covered nearly half the width of the US in a month before bad roads, burnt-out knees, an ailing bike and a backside that became redder than a Washington apple caused me to stop. Frazzled Americans would stop me and ask why I would do such a trip on a bicycle, and I'd tell them because my pogo stick was in the shop. There's no better way to see a country then pedalling through it. Planes, trains and cars move far too quickly and it becomes easy to miss too much along the way. I've found it's better to earn your destinations.

Travelling is one of the few things I'm good at and I've been doing it on my own since I was sixteen, to the point that my parents now refer to me as Marco Polo. Over the years I've come up with a few travel rules:

1. Always travel alone (it's really the only way).
2. Never trust a fat taxi driver in a poor country (same rule applies to politicians).
3. Look where all the tourists are going and head in any other direction.
4. Don't stay anywhere too long.
5. Never eat at a restaurant that has pictures of the food on the menu.
6. Pack light.
7. Meet people (these will be the memories that stay with you).
8. Always try to take the slowest mode of transport possible.
9. Never buy souvenirs (I have an attic full of junk to prove it).
10. Remember you're never lost, but you may not always know where you're going.

Apart from that, the world welcomes you with open arms, if you stay sufficiently broad-minded. If you travel enough it brings a peace of mind, knowing people are not so different whatever their corner of the globe. With that comes a sense of being at one with humanity. I guarantee you Napoleon would never have waged war across Europe had he gone backpacking when he was younger.

'This is going to be the trip,' my father said to me before I left. He had noticed every time I returned from a visit to Armenia I was always smitten with someone I had met there. 'I think we'll have a wedding to plan by the time he gets back,' he said to my mother, sniggering.

Chapter 2

Sweet Motherland

I like to see a city early in the morning. When the sun still hasn't had a chance to creep over the horizon and the streets are quiet, you feel it belongs to you for a short while, as you're the only one there, in that moment.

I began my day in the Hrabarag, a big open square at the centre of Yerevan. It has a fountain display of sapphire-blue waters at its heart and the grand archways of the Historical Museum, home to artefacts from the cradle of civilization. The architecture is sternly Soviet and on a grand scale. Government buildings faced with pale pink tufa stone surround the vast emptiness of the square. Its large roundabout usually bristles with traffic but this early there was next to no one, just street sweepers, hunched over, wiping away the previous evening's memories with straw brushes that were much too short.

Like most city squares, Hrabarag was designed to instil a sense of national pride in *Yerevantsis* and to make them feel small and in awe of the ruling power. Even though Armenia gained its independence from the Soviet Union in 1991, those Ruski habits still linger, the unshakeable curse on all post-communist countries. For years after Independence, taxi drivers couldn't find their way around the city because all the street names were changed from Soviet heroes to Armenian ones overnight and nobody could remember what the new ones were.

As I headed up Abovyan Street and turned towards

the imposing circular Opera House and all the outdoor gardens and cafes that surround it, I remembered being surprised at how modern it all seemed when I first visited the city years before. I simply hadn't expected to see nightclubs, or a waterpark, as everything I had ever learned about my country had been in the context of its history. At the back of my mind I replayed the joke that my grandfather liked to tell. A man of Armenian heritage arrives in Armenia for the first time in his life after years of dreaming about it. Walking out of the airport, he's inspired by the moment. He puts his bags down, falls to his knees and kisses the ground, exclaiming, 'My Armenia, my sweet motherland!' Only to turn around and see his bags are missing.

Yerevan is a modern-looking European city in many ways, but this can be a façade. Every city that prospers, every empire that's considered great, is constructed on the backs of an exploited workforce. Ask the slaves that built the pyramids, the Indians whose labour created the British Empire, the flood of American sweatshops in Asia, or the Russian man that was sentenced to thirty years of hard labour in Siberia for accidently breaking wind in front of a KGB agent. If you wander outside the centre of Yerevan, past the pretty gardens full of modern statues, further down from the five-star hotels, beyond the districts where you can order a cocktail next to a bubbling water feature, you will find nothing but Soviet tenement blocks built way too high for a country prone to earthquakes, and you will see the ordinary lives of the workforce who scrape by on a few dollars a day. Outside of the capital altogether there are a few small cities, but mostly there are only villages. Since the collapse of communism the factories have all closed, making it nearly impossible to find work. Armenians have been forced to return to the land and farm for their food. But even in the face of great poverty, they have retained their big hearts and their immeasurable hospitality, something I would come to rely on and greatly appreciate in the month ahead.

For a different perspective on this conflicted city, I climbed the Cascade, a monumental staircase complex with views of Yerevan and Mount Ararat from its summit. There are terraces at each if its five levels, dotted with sterile statues of odd figures that seem to have come from some alien civilization, and a water feature that was intended to 'cascade' all the way down but never worked. Near the top there is a museum that is seldom visited. This very expensive project has come in handy for one main purpose: it allows young lovers to climb to the high spots, away from prying eyes, and massage each other's tonsils. In Armenia people talk, rumours spread fast, and couples rely on the secrecy of dark corners and vantage points so high the in-laws would run out of breath trying to catch them. The final nail in the coffin for this folly is the ultra-modern home that occupies the hillside to the left of the steps; it's like something you'd expect to see on the coastal roads of LA's Malibu Beach. I always have a little giggle when I see it, as it's a very obvious sign that you are in a politically corrupt country, where taking bribes is common practice, as that's the only way a house like that could be built in such a location.

The view of snow-capped Mount Ararat from the top of the staircase is impressive, however. Although it is now on Turkish soil, some sixty kilometres to the south of Yerevan, Mount Ararat represents everything to the Armenian people. They believe, as in the Bible, that Noah's Ark came to rest there. Armenians call their country Hayasdan, derived from the name of Noah's great-grandson, Hayk, and see themselves as his descendants. That morning, the mountain was an especially strong presence against the cloudless sky. I watched as the slowly rising sun illuminated the waking streets and the first cars zoomed across the city. In a couple of days I would be cycling within close sight of the mountain myself.

* * *

At the Marco Polo Cafe that night, I met up with a group of friends for a farewell dinner. Marco Polo passed through the early kingdoms of Armenia several times during his travels. He was impressed by its cities and enjoyed its thermal baths, but remarked that the people drank too much, a fact unchanged. As far as I know, he didn't pass judgement on *basturma*, the potent, heavily cured meat that makes Polish sausage and Spanish chorizo look like infant children in comparison. Its strong pungent smell is a long-running joke among Armenians, but I had ordered a *basturma* omelette that morning and was now regretting it. It was the wrong choice for a summer's day, and for the next three days I smelled like I'd bathed in concentrated garlic and cumin.

It didn't seem to bother my friends though. They were more concerned about my trip. Jack, an Armenian friend from London, had been volunteering in Yerevan for the last four months on a tree-planting project. It was run under the auspices of Birthright Armenia, an organization that recruits volunteers from

8

all over the world to live and work in Armenia. But he sounded frustrated. 'In this whole time, I still haven't planted a single tree,' he said. His forehead was creased from widening his eyes in exasperation too many times and his large nose threw heavy shadows on the furniture. Jack had come to Armenia partly for work but also for love. He had met an Armenian exchange student while she was studying at Oxford University and had decided to come to Armenia to be with her and give it a try.

Also at the cafe were my local friends Suzie, Evalina and Nelli, all of whom I'd met at a village summer school where we'd been volunteers two years earlier. They were full of smiles at this reunion. The final arrival was Nayiri. I was looking forward to seeing her the most. She and I had met a year earlier, at Mount Rushmore. I was crisscrossing Canada and the US by Greyhound bus and had stopped off to join a tour to the Rushmore monuments. Also on the tour was a girl with a familiar-looking nose, and her name – Nayiri – confirmed my suspicions. We spent the day together and I promised I'd look her up the next time I was in Armenia.

There's a saying that wherever you go in the world you'll run into an Armenian. Our worldwide population stands at approximately eleven million, only about two and a half million of whom are in Armenia itself. The rest are scattered across every continent. When I sailed to the Antarctic some years ago, the ship's doctor looked up from his clipboard list of passengers and upon noticing my name immediately said, '*Barev.*' (Hello, in Armenian.) Great Scott! I thought. Even here. We later had countless vodkas together and talked about the old days. Armenians for the most part pride themselves on their adaptability and the ease with which they have integrated into their host countries. The various communities have a strong reputation as businesspeople, doctors, lawyers, politicians, artists, tailors and skilled jewellers. Our quirkiest hub is the city of Glendale in Los Angeles, where Armenian shops and restaurants line the roads. Every Armenian I've met has at least one relative living there. Muslims have their pilgrimages to Mecca, Armenians have theirs to Glendale.

So here we were a year later – in Armenia. Nayiri, with her long curly hair and Armenian nose. Armenians have prominent noses. A friend once assured me he could trace what part of the world someone was from purely based on their nose – a sort of Henry Higgins of rhinology. Nayiri and I were both a little surprised to see each other again. A year ago, she had been struggling with life in America, where she was lecturing at a university. She hated the food, couldn't get used to the people, and found things extra difficult during the harsh South Dakota winter, under two metres of snow. She looked relaxed and happy now, her face full of colour again, and I was glad to see her.

The drinks began to flow and so did the scolding. Everyone wanted to confirm that I was really going to cycle around Armenia. The warnings began: 'Watch out for snakes.' 'The uphills are treacherous.' 'Don't mess around or even look at the girls in the villages. Their brothers will kill you.'

Nayiri, an avid traveller and trekker herself, was the most encouraging and gave me advice on hikes I could take along the way. 'Just past the ancient temple in Garni,' she said, 'there's a walk to a beautiful waterfall.'

10

She hesitated for a second, and then said, 'But a tourist was eaten by a bear there last year.' I told her I'd skip that one.

I knew the ride ahead would be difficult. Earlier in the day I had met up with a man from the tourist board and showed him a map of my itinerary and the roads I wished to take. He sighed and said, 'I'd be scared even to attempt that with my car.' Armenia is mountainous, with very little flat land, so you're always going either up or down. The roads are pot-holed and you share them with drivers that all think they're in a Formula 1 race.

It was good to be among old friends before leaving. They all made me promise to send the occasional text so that they'd know I was still alive. I hate carrying a phone when travelling, but I take one for my parents so I can reassure them I'm still in one piece as they take a deep breath every time I announce my latest travel plans. But they're kind and they hide their fears well, no matter how crazy my adventure.

We said our goodbyes near the fountains in the Hrabarag as 80s pop music blared out to the rhythm of glimmering streams of lights. I walked Nayiri to the taxi station and, in my slightly tipsy state, thought about kissing her. I had just enough sense left to decide against it. I felt plenty brave but then remembered that stealing first base wasn't encouraged in major league baseball. She did look wonderful in the glowing streetlights on that warm summer night.

We found a taxi and she asked if I would like to come with her. 'My hotel's really close,' I told her. 'I'll just walk back.' In reality, I was ready to burst. I badly needed to find a toilet after all the bottles of Kotayk beer I had downed. We said goodbye and I went running back to my hotel, doing my best Usain Bolt imitation, feeling a bit foolish in the night. The next day, Jack explained that in Armenia men are expected to take a taxi back to the girl's house, make sure she arrives safely, and then head home themselves.

Chapter 3

God Loves Bicycles

From the first turn of the wheel nothing felt right. Two things were terribly wrong: I hadn't attached my pedals correctly and everything was way too heavy. Sure enough, within a minute of leaving my hotel, my left pedal fell off just as I approached the Hrabarag. I cursed in eight different languages and was angry with myself for not having done a test ride the day before. The thought of four flights of steps and awkward looks from the hotel staff had put me off the idea and now I was paying the price.

Pedal in hand, I walked up to a garden at the edge of the square, flipped my bike over and got to work. I saw that I had attached the pedal at an angle, an easier mistake than I thought possible, but a very silly one. In my one-minute ride I had already ripped some of the threads off the screw and it was going to be a tricky fix. Seeing me struggle, a taxi driver came over to ask if I needed any help. Meanwhile, a couple of drunken teenagers were swerving a new Mercedes around the roundabout in the empty square, listening to rap music, laughing their heads off. You can do anything in this town if you have money. I spent a good hour carefully fitting and readjusting until I had two very straight pedals firmly attached. In the back of my mind was the fear that I would get nowhere that day – or, worse, I'd be in the middle of Armenia somewhere and a pedal would decide to break off for good.

Pedals on, locked and loaded, I took my bike for a test ride to the other side of the square. Everything felt in good working order. My back tyre, though, was in a lot of pain. I sat on a bench, emptiness all around me, and thought long and hard. I had to shed the weight, and it was too late for me to lose ten kilos.

It was now 6 a.m., so I texted Jack my SOS plea, saying I needed to leave some things at his place. I was in a rush to get going and wanted to start on the open road. I was here to ride, to see my country and, possibly, meet the wifey if my father had predicted correctly.

'I'd rather cycle naked than leave my camera behind,' Jack said when he saw what I was intending to dump with him. I was frustrated and just wanted to leave everything and get started, but he reasoned with me. I kept the camera. He took a final picture of me outside his flat posing like a Greek Adonis, and then I rode off.

Everything still seemed a bit heavy, but not like before. The pannier bags attached to the back wheel felt balanced and were no longer about to burst. It was a relief to get started. After all the planning and the daydreaming about this moment, it was finally here. I rode southwest through the quiet streets of Yerevan, past the Ararat cognac factory – known for its fine brandy and for being Winston Churchill's favourite tipple, after Stalin introduced him to it – and then turned down Admiral Isakov Avenue, which leads straight to Etchmiadzin. Still the city slept and there were no cars to be seen. I had carefully planned that the first day of my ride would be a Sunday so that I could attend the 11a.m. service at Etchmiadzin Cathedral. I thought it would make a good start to a long journey. It was only a twenty-kilometre ride, which was nothing, but I wanted to do it early and miss the onslaught of tour buses and *Yerevantsis* that were sure to come to this most important spiritual centre, the Mother Church of Armenia.

I was riding down the quiet road admiring the view of Mount Ararat to my left when suddenly I heard howling. I turned to see a pack of four wild dogs rushing at me, looking rabid and hungry. I whistled and spoke Armenian to them in a soft voice, but that only seemed to make them angrier. They were vicious creatures with sharp teeth dripping with saliva and bloodthirsty eyes. They took position: one behind, one on my left flank, the other on my right and the fourth running straight in front of me. I had to brake hard to avoid hitting it. A collision would have sent me flying off the bike and quickly turned me into breakfast. After a bout of angry exchanges they eventually gave up and I was free to ride again, until the next pack arrived, and then the next.

I coasted downhill past the small strip of casinos between the city and the airport. These mini-casinos were like shacks and looked so barren and empty, like a forgotten little ghost town in the Wild West. Once past them, it was a nice easy ride into Etchmiadzin.

* * *

Etchmiadzin is like the Armenian Vatican: it's the headquarters of the Armenian Apostolic Church and the official residence of the Supreme Patriarch. The church is said to have been built in AD 301, on the orders of the saint Krikor Lusavoritch (St Gregory), and is considered to be the oldest cathedral in the world. As an early Christian in a pagan land, Krikor Lusavoritch was seen as a threat and was imprisoned in a deep well for many years. But he survived and went on to convert King Tridates III and the whole of Armenia to Christianity. The story goes that God spoke to Krikor Lusavoritch in a dream and with a golden hammer marked the spot where Etchmiadzin Cathedral was to be built. I wish God would tell me where to buy property and possibly which mortgage lender to use. But there's a good chance the story's false as excavations found that the cathedral was built on top of an earlier pagan temple. These days, Etchmiadzin makes a quick and popular day-trip from Yerevan for Armenian-American tourists trying to document everything with their hand-held video cameras.

The cathedral is constructed from smooth white stone, but age has added a layer of black ash, as though a fire swept over it. Its cruciform base is topped by several dome-shaped towers, like upside-down ice-cream cones, the largest of which houses the bell. The grounds are enclosed by fortified walls of beige stone. I found the gates, got off my bike and entered the compound. As soon as I walked in, a groundskeeper – tired and unkempt-looking – came running over in a panic, yelling, 'You can't come in here with that thing.' I was covered in sweat and dressed in full cycling gear and had no intention of entering the church until I'd cleaned up a little. I just wanted to see the exterior, now that I had arrived. I calmed him down and said, 'Don't worry, God loves bicycles.' He didn't seem to have much faith in that.

I retreated to a park bench in Etchmiadzin city to drink some water and think about my next step. An older woman with short white hair and a healthy complexion walked over to greet me, introducing herself as Gayane. She told me there was a hotel just outside town but that I should come over to her house first for coffee. She picked up her pail and led me to her front gate. I was barely able to squeeze my bike and saddlebags through it. We toured her garden, which provided the family with most of their food, and I met all of her chickens. Tomatoes and cucumbers, arranged in neat rows, grew all around, and overhanging grapevines and apricot trees created some pleasant shade.

As she set to work in the kitchen, I washed up a little and met her grandchildren, Gagik and little Gayane. I tried to ask them about their interests, but they were too fixated on the Russian-dubbed animation on the TV to answer. They occasionally gazed at me shyly to see who this stranger was. Their parents, Garen and Ruzanna, were more forthcoming. With a welcoming smile on his round face, Garen showed me the house, pointing out the various trophies and certificates his kids had won. He was in the army and was glad to be stationed close to his family, where he could spend time with his children and tend the garden. He asked about my trip and smiled when he heard about my cycling idea. Ruzanna immediately made me feel at home. She set the table and served me an omelette with a plate of fresh bread. 'The children won't eat the bread bought from the shop,' she said. 'They only like the bread I make at home.' When Gayane arrived with the coffee, we all sat around the table and talked about our lives until I sadly had to say my goodbyes.

As I left, I met Garen's grandmother outside feeding the chickens. She seemed a sweet old lady and spoke very nicely at first, but soon broke out into a rant out of nowhere about the lousy Turks. Garen simply smiled shyly.

The hotel turned out to be more like a row of modern apartments, each with a living space above a private garage. A man came out, a little alarmed to see me. He said I wasn't the first and that a professional Russian cyclist had stayed there a few months before. I went upstairs to wash and change into my best clothes for church: grey trousers, a black T-shirt, and the same black North Face trekking shoes I cycled in. I was happy to see that my bathroom had a perfect view of Mount Ararat. There was also a large living room, an adequate bedroom and a shower where the lever came off every time I tried to change the temperature. Still, it seemed clean enough.

The sun beamed down, emitting relentless pounding heat as I wandered through the gates of Etchmiadzin for the second time. The groundskeeper who had shunned me earlier was busy talking with an elderly man and pretended he didn't notice me. I wondered if he was considering putting a 'No Bicycles' sign outside the gate for future visitors. The crowds were gathering and I walked around the grounds looking at the ancient *khachkars*. These 'cross stones' are found all over Armenia in a tradition that dates back to the ninth century. Each *khachkar* is unique, the work of a master craftsman, but the principle is the same: a large rectangular slab of rock, engraved with a cross and carefully etched with intricate patterns. Some were used as tombstones and others for commemorating special events. In the modern day they are used as gift offerings: the Chinese give everyone pandas, Armenians give *khachkars*. Some are looked after meticulously while others litter the roadsides, abandoned and left to rot.

The scene inside the church was chaotic. It was as if we had all been invited to a wedding and every guest had been designated the official photographer. Tourists and locals alike were pushing their way through the crowds, camera flashes going off like at a football match just before a goal. So much for the 'No Photography' sign outside. The interior was stone, with a well-preserved painted ceiling, an exquisite dome and a pulpit lavishly festooned with golden knick-knacks. The priest could scarcely be heard amidst the scuffle and camera clicks. I chose a quiet corner and sat on a stone bench to take in the ambience, and also to avoid being pushed around by robust ladies that had once stood in Soviet bread lines and wrestled for a bread roll. Large religious paintings decorated the pillars and walls: worshippers placed their hands on the canvases as they prayed, touching the images of the saints and the Virgin Mary. I imagine the long-dead artists would be quite proud that their work was still getting such a lot of attention. After all, you never see anyone hugging a Rembrandt or cuddling a Picasso.

It wasn't just the paintings getting a onceover – a priest brought out a large rug hanging on a stick and the crowd went wild, running up to touch it. This kind of superstitious ceremony has always seemed ridiculous to me and I was happy to stay in my seat, especially when three beautiful young women came and joined me on the bench, dressed in their Sunday finest, all skirts and lace, long, flowing hair and dangerous glances. It was very warm in the church and as they cooled themselves with oriental fans, sweet lavender scent wafted off their warm skin and blew towards me. I began to think very unholy thoughts.

I lit two small yellow candles for my journey. One was for me and the other for Sayat Nova. I had decided to christen my bicycle Sayat Nova after the famous eighteenth-century musician and poet of the same name. Having fallen in love with the king's daughter, he was banished by the king and spent most of his life wandering through the villages singing his songs, which are still popular today. I thought my two-wheeled friend needed to exemplify that same spirit.

* * *

Back at the hotel, one of the employees invited me for coffee. The man who seemed to be the leader of the pack was gorging himself on a large plate of meat as the others watched. He had an angry face, spoke louder than everyone else and kept yelling out to the young kids, asking for updates. Every fifteen minutes or so a car would pull up with tinted windows and a man would jump out to ask about a room. The staff would turn to each other in confusion to check which room was free, take the driver's order for food and drink, and give him a spot in the garage.

This was no ordinary hotel, I quickly figured out. With old-time traditions still in place throughout the country, and most married couples still living with their parents and grandparents, young couples needed a hideaway. My hotel was born out of this gap in the market. And it was run like a mafia operation: the head honcho sat at his table keeping tabs on everything, some lackeys delivered the food and made sure they knew which rooms were free, and other kids were the runners who went out and bought cigarettes or anything else the young couples wanted. But the system was far from smooth. The whole process was more like a shouting match as the staff clashed over everything.

At night the place emptied and grew quiet. Presumably everyone had returned home to his or her scolding mother. I lay down to rest in my room and peered at my maps, looking forward to what daybreak would bring. And as I began to fall asleep, I thought how ironic it was that while I'd begun my day in church, I was spending the night in a love hotel.

Chapter 4

A Dalarik Soldier Returns

The Bible says faith can move mountains, but never mentions how a mountain can move men. I have rarely come across a geological feature so arresting, a peak that stirs the soul as much, a clump of earth that has left so many passers-by in awe of its beauty and its history, as Mount Ararat.

Not a soul seemed to be awake as I rode on to the main highway. I pedalled in careful rhythm, staring to my left where the mountain proudly stood, as clear and as close as I had ever seen it. Also to my left was the ancient site of Metsamor, which was first inhabited in Neolithic times and flourished during the Bronze and Iron ages (about 3300–500 BC). The people of Metsamor are said to have been the earliest astronomers, some 2,000 years ahead of the Babylonians. Much like in Egypt's Valley of the Kings, wealthy Metsamorians were buried in secret alongside treasures that would ease their way into the afterlife. Eventually the Urartu conquered Metsamor and later Armenian kings governed the area. The city continued to thrive until the seventeenth century. It was easy to see why early civilizations had prospered here, amid fertile agricultural land and with such grand views of Ararat. The nuclear power station to my right, though, with its large towers billowing smoke, seemed sorely out of place.

On the road I met a young farmer – tall and lanky with a big grin – whose first words were, 'Can I help you with anything?' He was walking to the nearby tobacco fields where he worked. When I asked which kind of cigarettes they produced he smiled broadly. 'Every kind.' The crops from the same field would later be used to make Marlboro, Kent and Lucky Strike cigarettes, or any of the other main Armenian brands. The tobacco all came from the same harvest, but the better quality leaves went into the more expensive brands.

I took the overhead bridge towards Sardarabad (the bridge was strangely Soviet in its over-engineering, like an LA freeway flyover, when all that was needed was a simple left turn) and hit a strong headwind, which made riding a struggle. I kept my legs pumping but felt like I was going half the speed I should have been doing.

Sardarabad, a grandiose war monument that honours Armenia's last stand against the Ottomans in 1918, consists of a tall staircase leading up to a twenty-six-metre-high arch hung with bells and flanked by a pair of huge stone oxen; the oxen are winged, being ancient protectors. It was a strange sight in the middle of nowhere, surrounded by dry, sun-baked fields. This was the battlefield that decided the fate of a people, the final line of defence to save a nation. In 1918, when the Bolsheviks took power in Russia, they pulled out their troops that had been protecting the Armenians. The Turks, who had come close to eliminating the Armenian people in the genocide of 1915, saw this as their chance to strike a decisive blow by taking Yerevan. Sensing danger, the head of the Armenian Church ordered that the bells of every church be rung to call on people from all walks of life to form an army. The bells rang for six days. From the shoemaker to the farmer to the poet, everyone united for a last stand. Here, on this field, the Ottoman army was defeated, only forty kilometres from the capital and what would have been the end of a country and possibly its people as well. The monument's bells are still rung every year to commemorate the battle. I placed Sayat Nova high up on the steps and photographed him in front of the monument, then sat for a while in its shade enjoying the quietness.

I rode back the way I had come, back to the over-constructed bridge and into the city of Armavir. This time I was flying: tailwind behind me, pushing me forward with ease. Armavir is highly industrialized; its small streets were heavily jammed with cars that kept nudging me over to the pavement. I decided to move on as quickly as possible.

Going by my map, I'd expected Miyasnikian to be a city; instead, only a few shops lined the main street and people milled around aimlessly in the midday heat, looking for something to do. I knew I had to turn off somewhere near the edge of town, but there were no signs at all. I asked a man if the road to my right led to Karakert and he grew very excited. 'I'm from Karakert,' he said, with a big smile on his bearded face. His name was Rostan and he was on his way to Yerevan for work. He asked to exchange numbers so we could have a beer when I returned to Yerevan. Over the next two months he called me nearly every day to check on me.

The land around me turned parched and desert-like and the road became a series of uphill stretches. There was nothing to see except for grey dirt and the occasional burnt-out Soviet tractor. The heat was excruciating and my legs were fighting the difficult gradients.

I was running quite low on water and energy reserves as I approached my fifty-kilometre mark for the day at the village of Dalarik. It seemed a pleasant place, with a row of homes along the main road and large stacks of hay piled up high. Just outside town I stopped at a small shop to get some supplies. It was run by welcoming, white-haired Garbis and his twenty-something son Sevag, who had a neglected beard and looked tired. They invited me to sit down outside the shop and rest. In the meantime, they examined my Giant mountain bike. Sevag stared closely at the modifications I'd made: the rack with double pannier bags on either end, the bar ends that stuck out like two horns to give me a second hand position, useful when climbing. It was as though I had landed on an alien planet and he was the first person to ask about the technology behind my mothership.

'What's this part do?'

'Those are the brakes.'

'How about this?'

'Those are the gears to make the uphills easier.'

'Like on a car?'

He enquired about the emergency tent I had in a small bag tied down with elastic cables and laughed at the idea that anyone would sleep in one of those. I offered him an English cigarette, which I always carry as a meeting tool, much like Native Americans would pass the peace pipe. Sevag gratefully accepted the gift and stored it away in his shirt pocket. He explained, with his father standing next to him, that he smokes but never in front of his father, out of respect. Garbis nodded, acknowledging that that was the system. Sevag asked what I was doing travelling in Armenia when there was nothing worth seeing. 'We work like slaves here,' he said, with a hint of anger in his tone. When I told him I was continuing towards Karakert, he kicked at the dirt around a pile of rocks and rusted steel and said, 'That's all there is in Karakert. What on earth will you do there?'

I decided to cheer him up a little and asked if he wanted to ride the bike. He looked at it worriedly at first, then hopped on and took it for a spin with a big smile on his face.

Garbis said it was apricot season and invited me to go picking later in the day. I was excited by the idea and said I'd love to. Sevag came back from his bike ride and asked if I would stay the night. Someone had just returned from army service and the entire village was celebrating. In Armenia, every eighteen-year-old male must complete two years of mandatory military service – a dangerous obligation. Although a ceasefire was called on the fighting in Karabagh in 1994, Azerbaijani snipers still line the border, taking pot-shots at Armenian soldiers. A former soldier once told me that if you lit a cigarette at night and placed it just above one of the defence walls along the border, a sniper's bullet would hit it almost instantly. For every soldier that loses his life, a small guerrilla unit is assembled to fight back and take a life in return. The war continues, but rarely gets into the news.

I thought this would be a good place to stop for the night, now that I knew there was a party. Garbis asked if I had anything to change into. In Armenia adults just don't wear shorts, so I went to the back of the shop and put on some trousers. We set off on a tour of the village, along a dirt path lined with small homes poorly constructed from cheap concrete and with slanting roofs. Village life is hard: tending the fields, taking care of animals if you're lucky enough to own any, and raising children amidst this poverty. But there was still a romance to the place, with its gardens full of vines, small vegetable patches and the smell of dung fires filling the air. I always feel most at home in this Armenia, drawn to the simplicity of village life. Villagers are the warmest of people, untainted by city ways. Though most of them have next to nothing, they will feed you and do anything they can to make you feel at home. Most are shy about their poverty and appearance, remembering that it wasn't always like this; once there was work and life wasn't as hard.

We passed a gleaming white, newly built school, financed by Armenian-Americans. Teachers are scarce as they rarely get paid, and few children pursue their studies for long; most, especially the boys, help work the land instead. I remembered how during one of my volunteering projects, a village boy of seven touched my hand and was in awe of its softness, claiming it was like a newborn baby's. He showed me his own already calloused fingers and exclaimed, 'You've never worked a day in your life, have you?'

* * *

Garbis's house was grander than all the homes around it, with a new orange-brick wall around the outside, tiled floors inscribed with vine designs in the front garden, and everything freshly painted in white. He had done all the renovations himself but his brother had paid, sending over the money from Russia, where he was working. Given all the smart new paintwork, I was surprised to see a bird's nest hanging off a light fixture in the hallway. Garbis smiled and said it was believed to be good luck if a bird decided to nest in your home.

Besides a manic-depressive son, Garbis also had two lovely daughters. The oldest was married; the youngest, who brought my coffee, wasn't. She was extremely eye-catching: petite, in her early twenties, with long, straight, jet-black hair and a face that was much too obviously beautiful. I tried with all my might not to look at her, so as not to end my visit in front of a firing squad. Or, worse still, married. One wrong look could have you standing in front of a priest in no time. I dared not look into her eyes; a gaze unmasks the soul, they say, and mine was dark and wrestling with thoughts about wrestling. In a village, you look, you like, the family likes you, and it's a done deal. There's no going for coffee or getting to know one another over a period of time. Much like in Soviet days, there's no time for window-shopping; you just stand in line and get what you're given. And for all I knew, she was a Phil Collins fan.

Many years earlier, when I was young and still very immature, I had entered into a dangerous liaison with a beautiful girl from the village of Saghmosavank, during another volunteer placement. Kristine captivated me with her piercing eyes and enchanting femininity. One dark night, with the moon shining through the trees, she took me by surprise and we embraced as the cool wind blew. The day before I was due to leave the village, she walked me to an ancient church, with her young cousin serving as a chaperone. As tradition goes, we stuck small stones into the walls of the church, and she made a wish that I'd return to her. She held my hand (our chaperone had moved location by then) and asked that I stay in touch. We shared a small kiss, which in a village can cause a major scandal for an unmarried woman, but we never saw each other again.

For the typical village man, courtship follows a predetermined course. Thoughts turn to marriage at the age of about twenty, once you've completed your military service. The rule is you never marry anyone from your village. You reach out to friends and relatives in other villages, asking if they know a suitable girl from a good family. A meeting is arranged. There may be several meetings. The girl may refuse, the family may refuse, but when all is well, the wedding usually follows quickly. A village woman is expected to marry by twenty-three; after that she's not trusted to have kept her purity, or may simply be regarded as having something wrong with her.

Garbis's lovely daughter would certainly be snapped up soon. In the meantime, she was busy producing a feast for her father and me. The table began filling up with an abundance of chopped tomatoes and cucumbers, fried eggplant dripping in oil, a large bowl of freshly made yogurt, various cheeses, fried potatoes and an omelette, all served with a mountain of newly baked bread. Garbis and I toasted our meeting with a few glasses of vodka. You cannot have a drink in Armenia without saying a few words first. You must give thanks for something, wish good health on someone, or just remark on the gloriousness of the moment. A simple 'Cheers!' (*Genats!* in Armenian) isn't enough. However short or long, there must be a speech.

Back at the shop, Sevag was getting ready to go to the apricot fields, but he decided I should stay with his father. Garbis and I sat outside and had a long conversation; in particular we talked about the Armenian economy. In the distance loomed an enormous abandoned factory the size of London's Battersea power station. It was once a wheat-processing plant, Garbis explained, and used to put the entire area to work. He pointed at another factory further to the left, which was where he had worked years ago. During the Soviet era, it was sufficient for only one member of the household to go out to work. Garbis had not only put food on the table but also saved a large amount of money for each member of his family. Then, in 1991, the Soviet Union collapsed and the money became worthless overnight. This caused trauma across the country and the repercussions were still being felt. It's hard to imagine an entire country losing everything at the click of a finger. Some people took to drink and never recovered, others returned to the fields and had to work hard just to feed their families.

Garbis was intrigued by law and order in England. 'You have rules there, and everyone follows them?'

'Yes, for the most part.'

'Not here,' he sighed.

The local government had recently fined Garbis because his shop was too close to the petrol station next door. He tried to explain that the petrol station had been built after his shop and that the government had allowed it to be erected there. But he wasn't given a choice – he still had to pay the penalty.

It was an interesting afternoon, with a lot of characters. An eighteen-year-old kid without a shirt on pulled up in a brand-new Mercedes, bought a beer, took a long swig when he got back in the car, and sped off. I have to share the road with these people, I thought. A middle-aged man did the same thing an hour later, except he was driving an eighteen-wheeler with a giant tractor on the back. For that kind of load, he needed two beers.

Then there were the 'confectionary mafia'. These were teenagers who travelled in pairs and turned up to collect money owed to them for ice cream, sodas and cigarettes. They worked for the companies that supplied the shop; this operated on a 'take now and pay us later' system and they were here for their cut. They all looked like heavyweights, ready to intimidate if they didn't get paid.

* * *

In the evening it was time to party, village style. We gathered in the front garden of a simple home. Garbis introduced me to the older men and said I was an Armenian journalist from England here to take pictures. (I had told him earlier about my job in TV, which involved me sitting around twiddling my thumbs, but apparently he wanted to show off his guest, and I was happy to play along). I shook hands with a number of heavily bearded men. Soon we got word that the food was ready and we piled into the house where three long rows of wooden tables were covered with food and drink. The men sat on one side of the room, the women on the other.

Garbis invited me to sit, but before touching any of the food, he reached for the vodka and began to pour. 'To meeting you and your health,' he toasted. I downed mine in one swoop and tried hard not to wince so that he wouldn't think I was a princess.

Our table of six continued to toast away and make

speeches as we passed around the various salads, cured hams and meats, a full array of cheeses, fried eggplant and three kinds of bread ranging from the very thin to the very thick. I tried to eat as much as physically possible, knowing full well my alcohol tolerance wasn't what it used to be. I tore into the Russian salad, hoping the creaminess would hold my stomach together. I thought of all the cycling training I had done, bullying my way through Richmond Park, and how I should have prepared by entering some drinking competitions instead.

Each drink loosened my newfound friends' inhibitions as they fired questions at me about English life and my trip.

'Are you married?' one man asked.

'What wife would let her husband ride a bicycle around Armenia like a crazy person?' I fired back, which raised a lot of laughter.

'Find a nice wife from here,' he said back to me, casually, as though he was suggesting I should pick up a postcard on my way out of town.

Just as I was about to ask Garbis about any Genesis albums in his daughter's CD collection, someone tapped me on the shoulder and told me to go take pictures of the *khorovadz* (barbeque). News had travelled fast about the visiting journalist. I found the women huddled over the deepest metal pot I had ever seen, loaded with thick chunks of charred pork and onions. It was beautiful. In the villages, meat is usually only eaten on special occasions. Animals are currency: I was told by a woman in another village that she paid for her son's university education in the capital by selling a cow a year. I tried to photograph the pot as the women shyly laughed in amusement at my efforts.

'This wasn't my idea,' I wanted to tell them.

The band – consisting of a keyboard player and a singer – began to play. The singer had a deadpan face with thick glasses and looked like someone who'd file your taxes, but he had a great voice and belted out Armenian party songs that all sounded strangely similar. Then in came the ladies, carrying plates of *khorovadz* high in the air, twisting and turning to the music in celebration of all things meat. This was the '*khorovadz* dance', apparently. I could get used to this sort of entertainment at dinnertime. Maybe finding a wife here wasn't such a bad idea after all.

The men cheered briefly but as soon as the plates hit the table the room fell silent and they began to feast. I chose the pieces of meat with the most amount of fat I could find, and I had them with thick chunks of bread to try to sober up. I wanted to be remembered as Garbis's honoured guest, not the funny guy from England who threw up in the garden. I really didn't want to drink any more but the shots kept on coming. People at the other end of the long table called me over to meet them, and more shots were poured until I started to make some grand speeches that were received with great cheers.

Khachik, father of the returning hero, also wanted to drink with me. I felt a little guilty because I wasn't even sure which one in the crowd was his son. But sure enough, Khachik got up to make a speech to welcome him home and yet another shot of vodka went down my throat. Then I did something only the drunken version of myself does: I danced. As drunken me often does, I thought I was magnificent and that my Armenian circle dance was an inspiration to all.

I liked watching Khachik. His son had returned and

33

he was filled with pride and joy. I have rarely seen such happiness on someone's face. Every time he passed me, Khachik would jump across the room, skip through the dance and throw me a big high-five, as if we had rehearsed this routine earlier. Garbis looked over at me and gave a big thumbs-up when he saw how well I was getting along with the crowd. The men mainly danced with the men, the women with the women. I had never smelled so much body odour in one place but it didn't matter.

I soon met the young soldier sitting with his friends and congratulated him on his return. I took off my necklace, which I had got in Peru – a *chakana* or Inca cross with a green stone in the centre – and gave it to him. I explained the mythology behind its design, how the stepped cross represented the Inca's tree of life. He wore it proudly and appreciated the gift. One of his friends turned to me and said, 'Maybe you can send me a gift when you get back to England.' I asked him what he had in mind. 'A Porsche Cayenne,' he said, laughing. 'It shouldn't be a problem for you.'

'I live in England but I'm not the *king* of England,' I told him.

We danced into the night, and Sevag joined us after closing up the shop. By 1a.m. most of the guests had left and Khachik invited me over for one last drink to wish me well. I congratulated him once again on his son's return and wished him all the best as we said our goodbyes. A final shot of vodka announced the night's end.

Sevag and I staggered back to his house. There wasn't a single light on alongside the dirt roads and I stared up at the stars as we walked. It was the most perfect, brightly lit night sky I had seen. The entire

Milky Way seemed so close you could touch it. Stars and galaxies always make me sad. It all seems too grand and infinite.

Sevag stopped me at one point and shined his phone on an open manhole warning me not to fall in. He moaned about his life in Armenia and his responsibilities and how, as the man of the house, he was forced to stay in Dalarik. He complained to the point that falling into a manhole started to sound like a pretty good idea.

He said he was concerned about his young sister marrying well. This perked me up a little in case I was brought up as a candidate. We reached the house, but instead of using the toilet inside we opted for the tree across the street. I've always felt there's no better way to confirm a friendship, a more primitive way of male bonding. We went inside and he showed me to the double bed we'd be sharing. I climbed in, exhausted, and he said I didn't have to keep my trousers on. Long-distance cyclists don't usually pack underwear as part of their gear, but I was too tired to get into that at 2 a.m.

Chapter 5

I Don't Have Any Pockets

As Sevag drove me back to the shop next morning, he began to explain why he hadn't taken me to the apricot fields the day before. He said he was ashamed, that their lives in this village were an embarrassment. He spoke of their poverty, the rags and hardships, and how the apricot fields were littered with snakes he was scared would bite me. 'There's nothing here,' he exclaimed angrily, bashing the dashboard.

I wasn't in the mood for his downbeat rants. I was too busy thinking what god-awful hangover music Michael Jackson was as it played on the radio. My head ached and my eyes were tired and bloodshot. The road was incredibly bumpy and my stomach took a beating with each jolt. I managed to make it to the shop with my stomach intact – and without violently shaking Sevag and yelling, 'Cheer up, you miserable sod!' I understood his discontent, but he had a wonderful family and wonderful people all around him in the village.

At the shop I gave my sincerest thanks to Garbis and Sevag and readied my bike. I was sad to leave them so soon. I needed water but I didn't buy any, knowing they would never let me pay for it. I had already enjoyed so much hospitality. A small group from the village gathered to wave me off with kind wishes.

Miraculously, I felt better as soon as I started to pedal. I rode for a few easy kilometres until I reached Karakert. Sevag, for all his doom and gloom, had been accurate in his description of the place. It was just dirt, rocks and rusted steel left to rot since the Soviet era. But it did have a petrol station.

I stopped to buy some bottles of water. Some cyclists use their own specially designed water bottles but I find that a two-litre plastic bottle of shop-bought water fits perfectly in the cage and you don't have to worry about washing it out on long journeys. A group of men sat in the shade in a small brick bunker while their cars were being refuelled. They seemed a little baffled at the sight of me but smiled when I started speaking Armenian.

'Don't your legs hurt?' one of them asked.

'Sometimes, but that's part of the challenge,' I answered. This was a difficult concept to explain in a country where the majority of the population struggled daily. Nobody understood why anyone would put himself through hardship by choice.

I picked up some bottles of water but was not allowed to pay for them. At first I thought my benefactor was the owner of the petrol station, but it turned out to be one of the customers, who insisted that the boss add the water to his bill. I was touched by his gesture. This big-hearted stranger had wanted to make a traveller feel welcome in this lonely spot. I wished the group of men all the best and they all wished me luck in return, waving me on in unison.

There were two roads to Talin. I chose the more direct one since it had an ancient fortress on the way, even though I had been told the surface wasn't the best. This turned out to be a gross understatement. The first few kilometres looked like a B-52 bomber had shelled the entire length of it. Luckily the road was quiet and I saw a car only once every half hour. At the end was a large climb with an extremely tough gradient. I felt like a bit of a failure not being able to ride it. My bike was too heavy and I imagine even a professional cyclist would have had some trouble with it (if they had drunk a bottle of vodka the night before). So I walked.

I enjoyed the quiet as I stared down at the rich green fields and farms in the valley below. I took one last look back at glorious Mount Ararat, knowing it would soon be lost behind the hills. Occasionally a car would pass and the driver would honk his horn at me. It wasn't clear to me whether this was an act of encouragement or the driver calling me an idiot.

Eventually I made it to the top of the hill, soaked in sweat that was probably a hundred per cent alcohol. As I wandered through the apparently lifeless village on the ridge, three kids came running over. 'Do you want to see Dashtadem Fortress?' one asked.

They led me through the village, laughing and joking, and up to the tenth-century fortress. Dilapidated but still magnificent, it occupied a commanding cliff-top position with an impressive view of the fields that stretched as far as the eye could see. An ancient wall surrounded the citadel, but many of the buildings had crumbled to dust. The castle keep, however, had been partially renovated. It was the size of a fairly large two-storey home, with thick orange stone walls, circular turrets and a collapsed upper floor. 'This is where the queen bathed,' said one of the kids, talking like an experienced tour guide as he motioned to a large opening in the middle of the floor. He took us up the caved-in staircase to the second floor and said his father had been the one to discover this route and that nobody had known about it before.

At the top of the staircase, a tumbledown wall gave us an incredible panorama of the surrounding landscape. Some ancient ruler must have stood there once, proudly confident of the castle's elevated position. It must have seemed impenetrable. We walked along the edge with nothing to stop us from crashing to the fields below.

Tour over, I gave the kids a few dollars each, making sure to explain that I wasn't just handing out money. Rather it was for the work they had done showing me around. They should continue to do the same for other visitors, I said. One of the kids laughed when he looked at the money. At first I thought he was calling me cheap, but then he said that the man in the middle looked like his grandfather. I would love to have met the George Washington of Dashtadem, but I had to ride on.

Stopping at a small shop on the edge of Dashtadem for a meal of crackers and biscuits, I found a seat in the shade outside. Three old men across the road were chatting loudly and I soon became the topic of their conversation. They made no effort to be coy and shouted out their every word.

'What's this guy doing with a bicycle out here?' one man asked.

'He's probably French,' the other said. And they carried on, trying to guess what I was up to. As I was preparing to move on, one of them came over and turned a little shy when I greeted him in Armenian. He told me how many kilometres were left to Talin, wished me well, and then scurried off.

The uphills continued. I sweated onwards, past a series of sad looking empty Soviet factories, finally pitching up in Talin, exhausted. I flaked out on a bench in the central square. The small hunched government buildings, purely Soviet in design, with stern lines and no signs of extravagance, seemed almost lovely coated in fresh white paint and a small fountain bubbled in the garden. Taxi drivers stared at me and talked loudly about this new stranger that had just arrived. I was given directions to a hotel two kilometres outside of town. It was deflating that I had to keep riding, but I decided to pedal hard and fast, motivated by the prospect of a good shower.

The small row of apartments, closed in behind a metal fence, looked more like a gated community than a hotel, but without the people. It was in the middle of nowhere, with nothing but empty parched fields all around and a busy road out front that was constant with traffic. Astghik showed me to a grossly overpriced room, but I was in no mood to complain. She was a woman way past her glory years and a little plump, but still seemed to be making every effort to recapture her youth. Her hair was an extraordinary shade of red, her nails long and garish, and her cleavage given much prominence in clothes that were far too small for her.

My room looked clean enough, the only problem being that both the living room and the bathroom had large windows but no curtains. I duly took a long shower where anyone passing could see me, and then ordered a large meal to replenish all the calories I had used up. I settled down to watch England play in the European Championships. I had 16,000 channels on my Russian satellite dish, but not one of them was showing the match. So I watched a Jim Carrey movie dubbed in Russian and learned he's not funny in any language.

***

Heading back into central Talin the next morning, I decided to give my legs a rest and take a taxi instead of my bike. My driver was an old man with a scrawny, unshaven face. When I tried to put my seatbelt on, he called out, 'No need for that,' as if I would insult him terribly if I insisted. After the first minute on the road I wanted to insult him many times over. He was a god-awful driver. He zigged and zagged around the potholes, not taking into account any of the oncoming traffic. I missed my bike and was relieved to finally put my feet on solid ground.

It was a pleasant sunny day and I went for a walk along the tree-lined streets. In the distance I could see an old Ferris wheel, now rusted away after years of neglect. Another reminder of Soviet days. People were busy shopping and discussing the latest news, but most stopped and stared when I passed by, knowing full well I wasn't a local. Armenians are never shy about staring. They will take a long hard look and won't even blink when you catch them at it.

A few cows mooed at me as I strolled around the grounds of Talin Cathedral, clearly irritated under the hot sun. The large domed basilica – minus the dome, which has long since collapsed – dates back to the seventh century. Its cemetery is dotted with ancient *khachkars*, but the modern tombstones were a far more eerie sight, with the faces of the deceased etched into the stone. As I entered the church gates, a small tour bus disgorged a group of middle-aged Italians who began taking pictures as if the cathedral was going somewhere. When I walked around to the other side of the building, I could see they had a point. The

41

entire back of the church had been completely destroyed by earthquakes, and the remaining shell was barely standing. The interior murals had nearly vanished with the decay of time and only the naked rock remained.

At the restored nineteenth-century church of Surp Gevork I got talking to a heavyset, slightly aimless-looking man who introduced himself as Levon. He had thick-rimmed glasses, stubble and a slow way of speaking and wore a striped shirt that didn't agree with his physique: all the lines curved over his stomach and made slopes. We went through the usual meet and greet, then Levon said I should see the ancient remains of the nearby chapel, bits of which dated back to the 1200s. He walked me into what looked like a gloomy old barn, full of heavy, blackened wood. At the entrance was a large stone stained with blood that looked like it was used to kill chickens. The air was thick with musk and the scent of melting wax. In the small prayer area, beneath a set of religious paintings, Levon explained the history of the church, mumbling big words I could scarcely understand. The ceiling hung low and sepulchral and the place looked as if it had remained untouched for several hundred years.

'How many people are in your family?' he asked.

'Four,' I replied.

He reached over, grabbed four candles, and handed them to me to light. I asked for one more: 'For my bike, Sayat Nova.' He laughed and said he liked the name. He bowed his head and recited a small prayer as the flames flickered in the stillness.

Levon invited me for coffee and we climbed the five flights of steps to his home. As he put the kettle on, I asked if he had a job, and he said no, there was

42

no work to be had. Was he married? Again, shyly, he replied no. He lived with his sister. We sat in the dimly lit living room on a long row of couches and he handed me a photo album of his army days. In the pictures he looked handsome and full of youth, a skinny figure with a strong, confident frame, quite unlike the rotund man he had become. I had thought he must be at least forty now, but actually he was not yet thirty-five. Life had been hard on him; it was obvious from the way he carried himself, head down and slightly defeated. There was sadness in his eyes. But he hadn't lost his warmth.

Back in the main square I found the skinniest taxi driver I could to drive me back to the hotel. I didn't even attempt a seatbelt this time, not wishing to upset him as he drove off like Evil Knievel. He had already heard that some crazy bloke had come into town yesterday on a bicycle laden down with bags. He filled the short drive with a long rant about all the problems Armenia faced. When I tried to introduce an optimistic tone, saying that I hoped things would improve soon, he sighed decisively and said, 'What's broken can't be fixed.'

At the hotel I ordered another large meal from Astghik. I noticed she liked me more now and, the more she warmed to me, the cheaper the price of the food became. When I paid for the meal she stuffed the money into her bra, laughing as she explained, 'I don't have any pockets.' She didn't have much space in her bra either, I thought.

After my meal she sat me down, adopting a serious tone of voice like she wanted to have a meeting. She started to discuss beauty products. All the products sold in Armenia were fakes, she said, and of very poor

43

quality. Did I have anything from England I could sell her? I was travelling very light, I replied, and toiletries weren't my specialty, but I'd see what I could find. I did have a men's face wash I wanted to get rid of anyway, to shed further weight off the bike. The inner child in me wanted to give her my chamois cream, which cyclists use to prevent bum sores, and to tell her it was the finest face scrub from Paris. But I knew I'd need it later. So I gave her the face wash, saying it was unscented so she needn't worry about smelling like a man. She was grateful and went running off to try it.

Turning on my phone that evening, I received a barrage of messages. Nayiri hoped I was well and looked forward to seeing me when I returned to Yerevan. I was still thinking about the near kiss a few days earlier and wondered if it would have resulted in a swift slap. There were five missed calls from Rostan, the excitable man from the road to Karakert. When I phoned him back, he was thrilled to hear about my progress but said he was worried and would keep checking on me. He told me to drink the water in Talin – the finest in all of Armenia, apparently. I did drink the waters of Talin, from a fountain outside the hotel, and they turned my own body into a fountain of sorts, right through the night.

Chapter 6

Do You Remember Me?

Bloody dogs, I thought, as the first pack greeted me bright and early, seemingly expecting me. This time the owner was nearby and, seeing me, called out to them in a booming voice, '*Khelok!*' (Behave!) This appeared to work as the dogs hesitated for a moment over whether or not they wanted to eat me. Maybe this was the way forward, I thought; it soon became my battle cry.

The ride started out easy, a downhill slalom between fields of glorious blues and purples. The farmers working the land looked at me with bewilderment. Some waved, some smiled and others just stared with a cow's fixed gaze. I reached the turn-off for the church of Mastara and stopped at a petrol station to examine the road. It was beat-up and harsh: the dirt and rocks would make riding next to impossible. It also would mean a two-hour detour, which my stomach, not yet recovered from the finest water in Armenia, wouldn't appreciate. I bought some drinks from the station and as I was gulping down a couple of tablets, I heard a young voice call out, 'Hello again! Remember me?' It was my little tour guide from Dashtadem. He was with his father now, who looked at me with a grin. They were off to visit family nearby. The boy was glad to see me and I him. It's always the random encounters that remind us of how sweet life can be.

I gave up on Mastara and instead continued on the

road to Gyumri. It was a long ascent and an extremely difficult gradient and I could feel every gram of my bike as I pumped my legs. But the higher I went on the dusty trail, the more my stomach began to ease up. I reached the highest point after an hour and felt a new energy with the promise of a long downhill ahead. I pedalled only once or twice and the road did the rest. The cool air hit me on the mountain pass as I swung down the bends, free to fly. I got down into my best aerodynamic racing position with my arms leaning forward on the handlebars, head down and bum high in the air to welcome the speed. I felt a great rush being in this landscape, with grass like an Irish dream, and I rode for all its beauty. I raced sharply down the violets and greens with my knuckles tense, drawing in the wind.

Down on the flatlands a tall young farmer held up a giant stick as I rode past and called out, 'Want a snake?' The large, brown, venomous-looking thing was still wriggling: it had been pierced right through the middle of its body. Further on, two farmers called out from a distant field that they wanted to bring me some water. But I waved a 'no thank you' in the nicest way I could and continued along the road, fearful of encountering other snakes in the field that separated us.

There were fine views of snow-capped Mount Aragats, then a mixture of easy flats and bad roads, and finally I came to the tree-lined streets of Gyumri. This used to be Armenia's second largest city, but in 1988 the region was devastated by a massive earthquake which killed 20,000 people and resulted in thousands of survivors leaving Armenia in search of a better life elsewhere. The population decreased dramatically. Aid flooded in and volunteers from all over the world came to live and work in the city. Nearly twenty-five years on, a number of internationally funded projects continued to operate in Gyumri, including at the school where my friend Arax worked.

Locals were quite used to seeing foreigners and members of the Armenian diaspora in their city. Sure enough, as I was pedalling furiously round a roundabout, a man shouted 'Bonjour!' at me. I would have got off my bike and struck him across the face with my cycling glove, challenging him to a duel at dawn for calling me a Frenchman, but I was too tired and near my destination to correct him.

A young kid on a bicycle was staring at me from the pavement, so I asked him which way it was to the centre of town, where I had arranged to meet Arax. The kid could have just pointed left, but he excitedly rode ahead to show me the route, enjoying being in the lead. He stopped only when my direction was clear, but before he strayed too far from home.

Arax was waiting for me as agreed. Years earlier I had promised to visit her city and now at last I was here. Her thick black hair had a few strands of white now, but her small tomboy frame and crooked smile were the same. It was nice to see a friendly face. We walked over to the school and children's community centre where she worked teaching art after hours to kids from low-income families. They could learn anything there, from music to photography, painting to filming. Arax had arranged a room for me on the top floor of the centre, which had been converted into bedrooms for visiting guests, rented out for a minimal fee.

There was an air of excitement at the school. The kids were staging a special musical event that day and they were busy preparing for it on the simple patch of grass that constituted the school's back garden. I got myself a drink from a refreshment stand that had been set up for the occasion and settled myself near the stage.

The singing started in off-key mayhem, but enthusiasm can make up for a lot of things. Almost as soon as the vocals began, the sky turned dark overhead. Clouds came full of menace and small drops turned to torrential rain in a matter of minutes. The sounds of laughing children filled the air and everyone ran inside.

I joined some visiting French kids of Armenian heritage who had gathered on the third-floor balcony. They looked like torn young things, all long hair, teenage angst and heart-felt music. Among them was a blonde girl who sat sulking and chain-smoking in the corner like she wanted to belong but didn't know how. One of the boys was playing AC/DC riffs and bungled solos on his acoustic guitar. It reminded me of when I was sixteen, full of Led Zeppelin but unable to play a single song to the end. My father, an accomplished tenor, tried to explain that a performance needed to be complete, to have an end, and that you had to make it clear to your audience when that was. I grabbed the guitar off the kid, who was in the middle of murdering the solo from *Stairway to Heaven* (as I once used to), and began to strum the opening chords to *Dock of the Bay*, the loneliest travel song ever written. Any traveller can relate to it: things left behind, an unknown future and being at peace with all of that. On the balcony everyone fell into silence with just the sound of my voice and the rain pattering down.

The local school kids had relocated to a small classroom for their concert. It was packed with way too many people for the space. We watched from the doorway as a young girl began to sing an Amy Winehouse song. Her shy eyes seemed afraid but she was enjoying her chance to perform. She sang brilliantly and fought her way through microphone troubles as the other youngsters listened attentively. I thought about the time I'd served Amy Winehouse a hot dog at a music festival on the Isle of Wight when I had a job in a food truck one summer. She too had seemed shy and afraid, but she'd been nice and had waited in the long line with everyone else.

There was a lot of happiness that evening in Gyumri: the excitement of the children and the flourish of song. The place was a real symbol of joy and hope in the city.

* * *

During the kids' concert a familiar-looking tall young guy with a gleaming smile came up to me. 'Do you remember me?' he asked.

'Saro,' I yelled as we gave each other a manly hug.

I had met Saro when we were volunteers together about eight years earlier and now here he was again, helping out at Arax's school. I hadn't heard from him or seen him since, but in a place where you didn't tend to meet many new people, it was easy to remember an old face. He was now in his late twenties, still with the same light hair, slightly Russian features and exceptional Armenian nose. He'd always had a very friendly way about him and it was easy to catch up on lost time. I asked about his sister, who I had once had a bit of a crush on, and was told she had married a Frenchman and moved to Paris. 'Good for her,' I lied.

Saro insisted that I go to his home for dinner that night. As the last of the day's light was fading we got into his Volkswagen Golf and drove through the streets of Gyumri. He pointed out the university where he had studied filmmaking and various other monuments around town. Whenever we drove past a church he would make the sign of the cross quickly, a purely Gyumri habit of superstition I was to find out. He stopped at the far end of Freedom Square and got out of the car to approach some overweight men wearing tracksuits. It looked like there was a drug deal going down, but it turned out he was actually exchanging money.

Saro lived in an apartment in the largest housing complex in the city, where 175 homes were clustered together. We greeted his mother and one of the volunteering French kids he was hosting. His mother prepared a grand feast that covered every inch of the table. 'I wish I'd known you were coming, I could have prepared more,' she said. The table remained abundantly full no matter how much we ate.

After dinner Saro showed me a short documentary he had made a few years back about the lives of disabled people and an organization that supported them. He wanted my opinion, knowing that I spent countless hours watching documentaries at the television network where I worked. My official job title was transmission controller, but that was too fancy a term for what I did, so I labelled myself a professional TV watcher. My job was to monitor the European channels playing out live on air and fix any errors, like missing languages or the screen going black. Most of the time nothing went wrong and I'd play on the Internet and make my next travel plans.

Luckily, Saro's documentary was good, real good in fact, and I didn't have to lie when I complimented him on it. It was very well shot and paced, but it was sad as all hell and made me want to cry. To lighten the mood, I put on some short travel movies I had made of Cambodia and Patagonia, which he liked.

We were both tired and Saro drove me back to the centre, playing bad Russian pop on his stereo.

Chapter 7

In My Grandmother's Footsteps

'*Yertank*,' was Saro's enigmatic greeting the next morning. Let's go. Without another word we got in his car and sped off.

He didn't tell me where we were going until a few minutes into the drive. The evening before I had mentioned wanting to visit an orphanage, and that was to be our destination. But first we had to stock up on traditional sweets.

We stopped off at a small market with a wall-to-wall display of candies, a giant pick-'n'-mix-style buffet of what Armenians call *confets*. *Confets* always come out when guests visit for coffee. Armenians prefer to take their coffee without sugar and to have it with one of these small sweets instead. The range of *confets* is huge – a vast choice of individually wrapped chocolates, toffees and caramels in any number of textures, flavours and combinations – but the colourful wrappers aren't labelled. You have to learn to distinguish between them through trial and error, playing your own memory game to recall which flavour comes in which colour. My experience with *confets* has always been very hit and miss, a lottery of pure chance in terms of quality unless you have in-depth experience in this field. Some can be tasty, while others you want to spit out straight away. This can present a big problem when someone has invited you over for coffee. During my trip I came to dread seeing these sweets on my host's coffee table. Many times I had to force down a disgusting *confet* so as not to cause offence.

Luckily, on this occasion I could make use of Saro's local knowledge. We amassed lots of bags of *confets* and also bought biscuits, wafers and boxes of bananas. Saro continually asked me if the price was okay and what my budget was and I told him not to worry too much. Then we were off to the toyshop across the street, where we haggled over balls, hula-hoops, colouring books, pens and stickers until Saro's car was full to the brim.

There was a special reason behind my wanting to visit an orphanage. My grandmother on my father's side (not the one concerned with my marriage choices) had been a saint of a woman and had dedicated the last years of her life to the children of Armenia. In her home city of Los Angeles she would spend the whole year collecting toys and raising money in preparation for her annual visit to Armenia. Then she would spend a few months visiting orphanages and villages all over the country, never letting weakness or fatigue get in her way. She was a woman of incredible faith and is remembered with great love by her family and everyone who met her. My brother and I made our first trip to Armenia as volunteers in her memory a year after she passed and her work has continued to be an inspiration on my every visit.

Although my grandmother was born in Jerusalem, her mother Haiganoush came from Sivas Sebastia, now part of eastern Turkey. The city was once a thriving place, with a population of approximately 200,000 Armenians. Then came the 1915 massacres and the beginning of the Armenian Genocide, during which the Ottoman army exterminated 1.5 million Armenians. My great-grandmother's entire family was killed. My great-grandmother herself was only saved by missionaries on condition that she became a Catholic. She was nine years old. She ended up in Jerusalem with my great-grandfather; he was originally from Tomarza, also in eastern Turkey, and had also been orphaned in the massacres of 1915, with just one brother surviving alongside him. These are not singular stories. Every member of the Armenian diaspora has horrific accounts of brutality and escape in their recent family history. And they are the lucky ones, with an ancestor that survived to tell the tale. Usually the stories are sketchy, vague and lacking in detail. Sometimes they are entirely suppressed. My great-grandparents' generation couldn't speak of what they saw, there were no words that would come to their lips, for what happened in 1915 was one of the most barbaric acts in human history. Silence shrouds the trauma.

My grandmother Marguerite and grandfather Hovannes married in Jerusalem and lived just outside the gates of the small Armenian quarter of the city where my father also was born. Marguerite and Hovannes worked as tailors until the Armenians got caught in the middle of the war between the Palestinians and Israelis. It was time to move again and, when my father was eighteen, newly graduated from high school, the whole family relocated to California. My grandparents started a new tailoring shop in Los Feliz, an affluent neighbourhood of Los Angeles near the Hollywood Hills. A lot of my childhood was spent running around their shop and eating the sweets that were kept near the cash register.

When my grandfather passed, my grandmother focused her time and efforts on causes close to her heart. My brother and I would spend weekends visiting her, but instead of sitting around the house watching TV, we would accompany her to elderly care homes, for whom she provided home-cooked meals. These meals didn't simply come in a large pot to be dished out to all the residents en masse, they were personalized and packaged according to what each individual liked, intricate dishes that took hours to prepare. I remember helping load crates of food in the boot of her car, her strong, thin frame lifting heavy boxes of wrapped Armenian delicacies, each labelled with its recipient's name. Then my dynamic grandmother would hunch over the steering wheel, getting honked at constantly for driving too slowly so none of the food would spill. She knew every one of the residents, and not only in one old people's home, but several. She would spend hours sitting and talking with them, listening to their troubles and giving them happiness with her kindness.

At a certain point she felt a calling towards Armenia, and in particular to the children of the country. She concentrated all her drive and energy on collecting all she could before her trips. I remember going to toyshops with her in LA and coming away without a single toy for myself. She would explain that it would be better if a little boy in Armenia that had no toys at all got one instead.

* * *

Saro and I pulled up at the orphanage in Gyumri. Large gates opened on to a courtyard that looked like the sort of place where Professor Xavier's X-Men might live. The Georgian-style mansion, built in dark stone and with pleasant gardens, was much nicer than anything I had expected. A few kids were playing outside; they were wearing second-hand clothes and gazed at us with shy expressions. A little blonde three-year-old was pulling a toy snake on wheels as a few older kids looked on. Some of the girls had their heads shaved – a sad and lazy way to prevent lice infestations – and I found it difficult to tell who was a boy and who was a girl.

We were directed inside and made our way upstairs, past several high-ceilinged classrooms and a performance hall, to meet the director of the orphanage. She looked tired but welcomed us and made time to tell us about the place and what they did. The fifty kids who lived at the orphanage ranged from three to sixteen, she said, but most were currently away at a summer camp in the forested area of Dilijan. She talked about the various circumstances that had brought the kids here. Some families simply couldn't afford a child; for others, a child born out of wedlock was deemed shameful and had to be given up. 'Some wake up crying when they've dreamt of their mothers in the night,' she said, teary-eyed. 'We have to console them with sweets or toys to bring them some happiness, and they feel all right again for a little while.'

The oldest girl, aged sixteen, was about to take her exams and would hopefully go on to university. When the boys turned eighteen they did their military service and might then continue with a career in the army. It was common for orphans to marry other orphans, we were told, though sometimes girls married outsiders, usually when quite young. I told the director about my grandmother and explained that my visit was an attempt to continue her work in some small way.

We walked back down to the car and two of the older boys offered to carry our boxes of gifts. We were introduced to the children, including a pretty-faced little eight-year-old girl who had arrived at the orphanage just the week before. I couldn't fathom who could abandon such a wonderful child. One of the older girls, Narine, had just returned from Paris, where she had given a performance on the *kanon*, an intricate stringed instrument, like a miniature harp, that she had learned to play at the orphanage. The director also explained that the children did paintings that were sold in America to pay the heating bill.

One by one the children recited poems and performed for us, while the teachers scolded them to be louder and interrupted every sentence with a remark. They were such great children and I began to find it hard to hold back my tears. What future would these kids have? Would they be able to find happiness? The director had told us to hand out the sweets ourselves, which we did, but I found it uncomfortable. It made me feel like I was some wealthy outsider giving out things to people lesser than me. These youngsters were really special and I wished with all my heart that they would have fulfilling lives.

Saro and I were silent on the ride back. My eyes flooded and I couldn't hold back any longer as tears rolled down my cheeks. When we told the girls back at the community centre in Gyumri about our visit, we were met with an angry response. 'You gave everything you bought to the principal,' they said in frustration. 'We took things there last week and the kids didn't see any of it.'

I shrugged. If that was the case, it would be a moral tragedy, but in the end it's not material things that count. A toy or a sweet is inconsequential. It's your time and the positive influence you have on someone that makes a difference in peoples lives. My grandmother always understood that. But still it's an Armenian tradition never to turn up empty handed, and I hope in the future I'll be able to spend more time with the underprivileged children of Armenia, just as she had done.

Chapter 8

A View Of The Past

I didn't grow up hearing fairy tales. The stories I heard as a child were of unspeakable violence, of grotesque mass murder, and they were the true stories of my people. They were accounts of what is often referred to as the First Holocaust when, in 1915, Turkish officials ordered the complete extermination of the Armenian people. Armenians lived as second-rate citizens under the Ottoman Empire, which at that time extended from Istanbul to Azerbaijan. They represented about 10 per cent of the population and, being Christians and successful tradesmen, became the targets of persecution. When Armenian leaders announced that they wanted autonomy from the Ottoman Empire, a self-governing republic in the east, they were instead handed a death sentence.

It all began on 24 April 1915 when 250 intellectuals and high-ranking Armenians in Constantinople were arrested, jailed and later killed. From that point started the systematic eradication of the Armenian population of eastern Turkey. The men of each city and village were rounded up and taken away for immediate execution. The women and children were led on death marches into the deserts of Syria. With no food or water, thousands died of starvation. Others died of asphyxiation when they were forced into smoke-filled caves, a primitive form of the gas chambers later used by the Nazis. Many more were tied together and thrown off cliffs to drown in rivers that turned red with their blood. In some places the bodies piled up so high that the river changed course; to this day people refuse to drink from those rivers. The most horrifying image from my childhood, the one I still can't get out of my head, was a picture from the archives of a row of women crucified naked on a line of crosses.

Several German military officers were stationed in Turkish regiments at the time and witnessed the mass killings; they later became high-ranking officers in the Third Reich. Rudolf Hoess was one of them. He served with the Ottoman Sixth Army and years later, in 1940, was given command of Auschwitz. Hitler himself was all too aware of the links. Looking to justify the Jewish holocaust, he asked, 'Who, after all, today speaks of the annihilation of the Armenians?' He thought that the systematic murder of 1.5 million Armenians could be ignored. Shockingly, others have echoed this view.

The evidence of these crimes is monumental. There are comprehensive written accounts from witnesses, a library of photographs, and survivors who have told their stories. There are caves and dried-up rivers that are still full of corpses. It might sound morbid to tell these stories to a child, but it was essential that they be remembered because to this day the Turkish government denies that these events ever took place. They are not alone. For years America has bowed to political pressure from Turkey not to recognize the genocide; in return the US has been allowed to house military bases in Turkey and given free access to air space when searching for Arab oil. Even Sylvester Stallone has felt the heavy arm of Turkish politics: pressure groups scuppered his plans to film Franz Werfel's 1933 novel *The Forty Days of Musa Dagh*, which was inspired by the true story of a city that heroically defended itself against the Ottomans. This denial policy is well orchestrated and funded; it uses blackmail and threats. Schools in Turkey have reversed history in their textbooks and as part of their curriculum teach that the Armenians massacred the Turks. Surprisingly, Israel is another on the list yet to recognize the genocide; the one place you would expect to be more sensitive to such an issue.

When you listen to just one Second World War holocaust denier arguing his case against a person of Jewish heritage, it seems ridiculous enough. In the case of the Armenian holocaust, entire countries refuse to acknowledge the facts about the near extermination of the Armenian people. When you understand this, you begin to understand the plight of the Armenians.

There is anger and frustration in all these matters, but it's important to state that this is not directed at everyday citizens. I have Turkish friends, some that are like brothers to me, and there is a Turkish kebab shop down my road in London that would have long ago gone out of business had I not been its best customer. It's the cowards behind desks that I have hatred for; those who are mad with power, those who pursue the politics of greed, those in high places that are so afraid of their own mortality they search for legacies abandoning any sense of morality. On their watch, it's the people that suffer.

* * *

Such thoughts weighed heavily on me in Gyumri, being just a few kilometres from the Turkish border. While I was in the city, Jack turned up from Yerevan with a busload of Birthright Armenia volunteers in tow, wanting to visit the border. I agreed to go along and we all met on a barren piece of land a thirty-minute drive southwest of Gyumri. A large Soviet-looking mustard-yellow bus was waiting to take us through the army checkpoint near the border. There wasn't enough room to sit, and some of us stood as we bounced and rolled along the dirt track. I got the spot next to the large fuel cylinders at the back, which made rust and dust stains all over my trousers. We rocked and rolled, with laughs and yelps, until we reached the large barbed-wire fence of the army post. With this in our sights the mood turned decidedly solemn.

Some soldiers opened the gates and led us through, and we were given instructions on how to behave in the border zone. From our cliff top vantage point we looked down into the gorge far below us to where the Akhurian River divided Armenia from Turkey. On the other side of the vast gorge was the ancient city of Ani, which flourished in the tenth and eleventh centuries as the capital of the Armenian Bagratuni kingdom, when it was known as the city of a thousand and one churches.

I had never been so close to the land of my ancestors. The dry red desert in front of us, peppered with the crumbling mortar of a few half-standing churches, like a vast tomb that had been plundered. I tried to imagine Ani as it once had been, rivalling the greatest cities in the ancient world with a population of more than 100,000, but it was difficult since there was very little to look at. The Ottomans stole most of its religious artefacts, some of which were the earliest Christian relics in existence (the few remaining that were smuggled out are now in Yerevan's History

Museum). In 1921 the Turkish government ordered the complete destruction of the city. For years it remained a military zone, a heavily guarded no-man's-land. But more recently, since Turkey has sought to join the EU, it has allowed tourists to visit the handful of dilapidated structures as a sign of its goodwill and modernity.

Beyond this gorge was the history of my people: beyond Ani and into the distance. What made me saddest was that I had no knowledge of what life was like in the cities of Armenia before 1915. My great-grandparents were rendered silent by the traumas of the past and the stories were all lost. People laughed and loved there; others hoped, others cried. The lineage that led to me, the habits and traits that still linger, born there in front of me, were cut at their roots, never to be remembered.

The group watched over the expanse, each with their own sense of loss, as silence fell on us all.

Chapter 9

Changing Light Bulbs

Women strolled the streets of Gyumri in chic Buenos Aires-style fashions and high heels, quite possibly the highest heels in Armenia if anyone cared to do the statistics. Few of the pavements were level and this made for some impressive balancing acts. It reminded me of when I visited the Buddhist monasteries on Mount Emei in the Sichuan province of China, where Chinese ladies raced up the rugged dirt path in their heels, refusing to allow the rough terrain to stop them from looking taller or in fashion. The gleaming white government building in Gyumri's grand central square was also rather incongruous. Its White House-style design, complete with semi-circular domed centrepiece and endless pockets of windows took up an excessive amount of space and seemed over the top for such a small city.

Much more typical of 'Leninakan' – as the older generation still call Gyumri – were the old men who sat in one of the city's many parks playing cards as though they hadn't moved for forty years. The nearby Ferris wheel looked equally venerable. It was still in operation but made certain noises that suggested it should have been shut down long ago. Naturally, I purchased a ticket, nervously excited by the death trap. The white wheel moaned and groaned as it trudged through its rotation, lifting me high above the tree line and affording expansive views of the city and beyond. At the city's limits I could see the statue of Mother Armenia, dedicated to all those who lost their lives in the Second World War. On the back of the statue, facing Turkey, was carved a jackal with aggressive features. Just below it snaked the same gorge that continued to Ani and made a natural border.

At the market, old ladies argued over prices and nothing could be bought without a shouting match. Along the crooked path men sat swatting flies off the meat with tasselled sticks. An old, frail man approached me and asked if I could help get him his deserved honours from President Sarkissian, which he had never received after the Karabagh war. A few young men behind him began to laugh, and I said as nicely as I could that I couldn't help.

Inside the ash-grey stone walls of the Cathedral of the Holy Mother of God, with its cruciform shape and large conical dome, I heard the songs of my childhood. The *Badarak* is the traditional Armenian church service of songs and prayers, sung in Armenian churches all over the world and one of the earliest surviving Christian ceremonies still in existence. In my youth the songs used to bore me to tears, but now I only felt nostalgia. The church was crowded, with very few pews for sitting. The stereotypically fat priest with a heavy beard was dressed in green and gold cloth. He performed his duties with great precision as one of the younger priests swung a metal pot back and forth spreading the scent of incense with puffs of smoke.

There is a long list of rules to follow during church ceremonies, all of which I used to try hard to break as a kid:

1. No talking or chewing gum.
2. Don't look behind you away from the altar.

3. Never clasp your hands or place them behind you (this is seen as an act of revulsion).
4. Never place your arms over the back of the pew in front or cross your legs.
5. When you enter the church you must cross yourself, and you exit the church the same way, only walking backwards while bowing (this last part can be very difficult and you always end up bumping into someone).

The most difficult thing about attending these services is to know when to sit or stand. You're allowed to sit down after certain songs and prayers, but people never remember which ones, so they wait for the priest to motion that it's okay and that's when you hear the collective groans of relief. I like the ingenious system employed by a church in Montreal I attended once: they had a cross at the front that lit up when you had to stand and went dim when it was fine to sit again.

Among the congregation at Gyumri's cathedral I spotted a familiar face – it was Arman, whom I had met the day before with the Birthright volunteers on our trip to the border. He had just arrived in town and was being dragged round to all the sights by his new host family. Later he'd be taken on a picnic and be force-fed pork all afternoon. He looked at me with a glimmer of hope that he might escape, but we both knew he had no chance. You have to love Armenian over-hospitality.

* * *

After the service, I met up with Arax and we took a taxi to Marmashen, a tenth-century monastery complex located ten kilometres north of Gyumri in a low-sided valley with a river running below it. Inside the beautifully preserved main church, beneath its umbrella-style dome, I lit a candle for each family member. There were originally four churches on the site, but a series of conquerors and earthquakes has left most of the structures in ruins. Beyond us on a ridge a piece of wall about three metres high and just as wide was all that remained of what must once have been a magnificent church. The building that housed the monks was also now just a rubble of stones. Fine cross carvings and biblical inscriptions lay scattered around the site atop fallen walls.

Back in the city I joined the Birthright volunteers on a visit to Gyumri's Black Fort. The fort is completely round, made of dark stone and set on the side of a hill. The Russians built it in 1837 as a defence for the city against the Ottoman Empire. I couldn't understand why anyone would bother trying to capture it, and not just walk around the thing to take the city. I guess old armies were sentimental that way. Inside, everything was in a state of ruin, overgrown with weeds and littered with rocks that we had to clamber over. We scaled the walls to get a soldier's perspective. Below us on one side stretched the rooftops of Gyumri, and on the other side was Turkey, across the wide gorge.

We marched further up the steps to the Mother Armenia statue and opened the shopping bags for our picnic. We accidentally interrupted a young couple seeking privacy on the Turkish side of the statue underneath the carved jackal. Better that your political enemy see you in his sniper's scope than your future mother-in-law, I thought.

In the main square a stage had been erected and the place was full of life. It was graduation day for the city's students and everyone was celebrating together. Music was playing and it seemed as if the entire city had shown up for the occasion, dressed in their finest attire, ready to congratulate the happy students and their proud parents.

Back at the centre, Gago, the school's well-groomed white-haired caretaker, told me about the time he and his rock band had played an unofficial gig in the same square – some twenty-five years ago, in the days after the earthquake of 1988. Gago had a childlike smile that you could tell liked trouble, and with one eye a slightly different colour than the other, you knew he had seen some. He took out his phone and began playing a heavy rock track. Bobbing his head to the beat, looking at me to see if I liked it, he beamed. 'That was my band,' he announced. He and his friends had started the band partly to make money but mostly because there was nothing else to do. For their gig in the square, they had all dressed in black and had put on a good show, but then they were arrested. He smiled at the memory.

In the evening everyone from the centre gathered for a goodbye party at a restaurant that had a tacky Las Vegas feel to it, with garish pink pillars and a full-sized standing stuffed bear at the entrance. I chose a Georgian dish with layers of mushrooms and sliced pork topped with heavy cheeses. It was delicious, but halfway through I couldn't take in any more and waved my white flag, though in this case it was a hot pink napkin. Speeches were made as we all wished the French volunteers well.

Anna came and sat next to me. She had the raw

beauty of an Oklahoma sunset. Her fiery manner conveyed an excitement for life, her vibrant personality resonating in the twinkle of her eyes. She spoke of how she loved being a volunteer in Gyumri but that soon she would be returning to her life in France. As she nursed her bottle of beer she scratched the paper label off and broke toothpicks into small pieces. I told her that in England we'd view that as a sign of fleshly frustration. She laughed sweetly and said that wasn't far from the truth. Her hair of golden sand was done up in a bun exposing her long slender neck of perfect skin. I was worried about my attraction to her, having already previously dated two girls named Anna. One was quite possibly the sweetest and the most wonderful girl I had ever met; the other was the whore of Babylon.

'We need more vodka!' Anna announced, as we went out to have a look at the fridge. We decided everything on display was equally disgusting, and given that neither of us were connoisseurs, any one of them would do. The bottle we chose was called Alexandrapol, an earlier name for Gyumri from when the Russians had been in power in the nineteenth century, named after Tsar Nicholas I's wife Alexandra. We toasted our meeting, and continued drinking till we were brave enough to join the rest of the group already up and dancing.

Anna said she didn't know how to dance to Armenian music. The concept was quite easy, I told her. 'Just change the light bulbs.' I raised both hands in the air and moved them in little cupping twists. She broke into a fit of laughter at this and we both hopped around pretending to change light bulbs in the most inventive ways possible. We changed light bulbs behind our backs, under our legs, and even helped the other with their own bulb. Vodka had fuelled our spirits, but the scent of her perfume had the most sobering presence every time she came near me. We drank and danced to the night's end. Tomorrow she'd be on her way back to France. She didn't believe in goodbyes. 'See you soon,' she said with a large smile.

Chapter 10

The Only Cyclist In Spitak

After a few days' rest it was time to ride again. The nice old lady who took my order for coffee looked at the maps spread out in front of me and said, 'All of Armenia's the same. Same people, same things.' While I mulled over possible routes, a pretty young waitress turned up for work full of seductive smiles and a very obvious hatred for her job. She'd take an order, then play on her phone, then the old lady would call her inside and there would be a loud shouting match. This was repeated several times during the hour I spent there, and I watched, fascinated, like David Attenborough observing some rare species.

It looked like I was going to have to re-route. I had been considering heading further north towards Lake Arpi, the main reason being because I'd never heard of it, but everyone I asked about this said the roads were awful in that direction. I decided to cut east instead and head straight for Spitak.

Outside Gyumri's city limits, I reached an open valley naked to the winds that began to go against me. Progress became painfully slow, even when I reached a downhill. I had to work hard and fight for every metre. In the distance I could see what looked like a city and the outline of buildings, like a mirage. As I got closer I realized it was actually a cemetery with tombstones covering the hillside. A lot of the graves were likely to have been from the earthquake, when the city burial grounds couldn't cope with the numbers. It was a meaningful reminder as I headed towards Spitak, the epicentre of the quake.

I began to climb and climb up a difficult slope with the winds still pushing me back as I passed over a ridge between two cliffs. At the very top of the climb was a large *khachkar*. I stopped Sayat Nova for a picture and stared at the downhill that lay ahead. The wind had eased by now and I crouched into my best racing position and began to fly down the road. I turned smoothly with every bend as the air buffeted my face and I rejoiced that the climbs were over. Even the most difficult terrain is quickly forgotten on a nice downhill ride.

In the village of Lusaghbyur I stopped at a tiny roadside shop no more than four steps long from end to end. It was run by the lovely and aptly named Siroushig: 'Little Sweetness'. As I was picking up a few biscuits and water for breakfast, a man came down from the fields and tried to add another beer to his tab. It was 10 a.m.

'How many have you already had this morning?' Siroushig asked him.

A childlike grin spread across his craggy face. 'A few.' He explained that a woman in the village had passed away the night before and that he had been digging her grave. He managed to bargain a beer using his most convincing tone of voice and drank it down thirstily like a college student. He asked if I wanted one too and I told him I had to ride straight for the rest of the day.

Siroushig's son Edgar and his wife came in, and immediately offered me coffee and sweets. The little *confets* were absolutely awful but I appreciated their generosity.

'Why aren't you married?' Siroushig asked.

'Because nobody's proposed to me yet,' I said in a sad voice.

They laughed and mentioned they knew some girls in the village, if I was interested.

I was outside preparing the bike, with my newfound entourage looking on, when a nicely dressed older gentleman approached us. He was wearing a plaid shirt underneath his coat, well-ironed trousers, and a Chinese designer belt. He spoke very eloquently as he welcomed me and shook my hand. He then drew closer and pointed to the inside of his jacket pocket, asking in a low voice if I'd like some vodka. Just as he did so, a mini bus rumbled up the road and he began frantically waving it down and running after it, screaming for it to stop. The bus slammed on its brakes and skidded some distance past the shop as his panic subsided before boarding.

Past the village were large plantation fields. I did a double-take when I noticed the people working in them appeared to be dressed in the colours of the Armenian flag. Four were wearing red, four blue, and another four orange and they walked in formation, ploughing the earth. It was a strange sight, and I thought it was a coincidence until I took a second look. I tried to imagine what sort of landowner had come up with the patriotic dress code.

From my map I knew Spitak was close, but I was disheartened when I realized I would need to go through a tunnel to get there. When I reached the mouth of the tunnel, two guards pulled me aside nicely and said I should put on some lights and be very careful when riding through, as it wasn't lit. Portly, proud-faced Hratch had lost his right arm; he shook my hand firmly with his left and invited me to the guard station for *sourj* (coffee). The other guard, Armen, was young and inquisitive as we sat in the office. We talked about the recent mass exodus from Armenia, how everyone was leaving in search of a better life elsewhere. Hratch was dismissive of this, saying opportunities were there for the taking if people wanted them enough. They were both impressed by how well I spoke Armenian, and said they thought most people in the diaspora could barely speak a word.

Inside the tunnel I could hardly see a thing. I had fastened my bright headlamp to the back of my pannier bags and gripped my emergency mini flashlight, only the size of a pencil, to try and illuminate the way ahead. I nearly hit a large beer bottle that could have sent me tumbling, but I saw it just in time and swerved away. After a few minutes, which went by painfully slowly, I finally saw daylight and pushed hard as the cars flew past me. Out on the other side to my right was Spitak.

The centre of the city was bustling with people doing their shopping and generally milling around. Only a small government building marked the city square in this almost picturesque place surrounded by green hillsides puffing with smoke from the scattering of villages beyond. I pulled my bike over to ask three teenagers if there was a hotel in town. They said to follow them and they'd show me to the YMCA. None of them wore yellow hard hats or sported moustaches so I decided to go along.

It was a great recommendation. The YMCA was new – built after the earthquake with Swiss funding, to provide activities for the youth of the city – and set in leafy surrounds on the other side of a lake. It had a sports centre with football, table tennis and gym facilities, plus a puppet theatre and a wonderful kindergarten busy with shy youngsters who all greeted me when I was shown inside. Staff member Grisha checked me in and welcomed me like family; his face wore a constant smile. As we passed the computer room he introduced me to an elderly lady who was learning to use a computer for the first time. 'Look, she's sixty, every age can come,' he said proudly. He then directed me into a classroom where three teenagers were learning English. Their teacher, Lena, caught my attention immediately: mid twenties, black hair tied in a ponytail, glimmering dark eyes that could move mountains and small stars dangling from her earrings. She had a face full of kindness and a graceful, petite frame. It's so easy to fall in love in Armenia, I thought. I spoke to the students in English in an attempt to impress the teacher, and they responded shyly, with confusion on their faces. 'Right, let's go!' Grisha called out, to my great sadness. I wanted to stay with Lena and discuss her abbreviations and conjugate her verbs but it all ended as soon as it had begun.

Grisha was excited to see my bike. 'You know, I'm the only one who rides a bicycle in Spitak,' he said as he showed me his bike parked in a shed at the back of the building. It was a simple green bike from some unknown Chinese manufacturer but it made him beam with pride. He examined my bike with great care and admiration. I told him to take it for a ride, and he hopped on, whooping and hollering as he went. His friends came outside to see what was going on, and a lot of laughter filled the air. He loved the feel of the bike and the fact that it had gears. I felt a brotherly love for Grisha immediately. He had such a soaring, happy spirit.

'Whatever you need while you're here, we'll help you with it,' Grisha said back in the office. 'Are you married? Be at the church at 10 a.m. tomorrow if you're not, we'll find you someone.' Everyone in the office laughed. I said I'd be there, and that there would be no need for a limousine, we could simply put a 'Just Married' sign on the back of the bike along with some tin cans before riding off into the sunset. Grisha wasn't married either, and I suggested holding a double wedding.

My room at the Spitak YMCA was immaculately clean with soft bedding and a shower so hi-tech it would have taken a user manual of biblical proportions to figure out. There were buttons for different lighting, pressure and heat settings, radio, and there were eight possible directions for the water to come out. I don't go searching for too many comforts when travelling, luxury usually brings about complacency and boredom, but a good shower at the end of a hot ride is a wonderful thing. The fact that I got to push a lot of fun buttons while doing so was a real bonus.

I took a walk around the city, through the square and alongside the church. The quake had turned this once vibrant city into a village. There were a few new buildings, but many scars still remained. Some say that 90 per cent of the donations sent from overseas to help rebuild Spitak went straight into politicians' pockets. People stared at me as I walked down the street, likely because I was wearing a peach-coloured shirt with a bicycle on it. Bright colours on a man are rare in Armenia, and cycling is seen as something only for children.

I returned to the YMCA just as the staff were finishing their working day and saw that they had prepared a table brimming with pastries, sweets, coffee and wine to welcome me. Lena sat across from me as Grisha raised his glass to toast: 'Life…. is like…' and he launched into a long monologue full of illustrious clichés. He paused and we thought he was finally done, but then he resumed: 'Life… is like a gift…' He continued on bravely in the face of repeated attempts to shut him up, comparing life to bicycles, worn shoes, and open roads. Eventually he was forced to draw his speech to a conclusion and we all drank. The pomegranate wine was as sweet as syrup, the food was grand, and the reception I was given will forever make me smile at the memory. I stared across the table at my newfound friends like a family that had adopted me as one of their own. Lena was truly beautiful. They all were.

Chapter 11

I Only Eat Ice Cream

In the morning all the YMCA staff gathered round the table again, this time to celebrate the birthday of the son of one of the employees. 'It's nearly ten o'clock!' Grisha shouted. 'You need to be at the church for your wedding!'

'I'm ready. I even got up early to do my hair,' I said, brushing my hand across my bald head. I told them the story about my uncle who was notoriously late for everything. When his niece was getting married, the family told him the start time of the wedding was an hour earlier than it really was. For once in his life, my uncle turned up on time, saw there was nobody around, figured he had the wrong weekend, and went home.

It was time to say goodbye. I readied the bike and gave Grisha one last big brotherly hug. All of the staff assembled outside and waved me off with a big fanfare. My time there had been too short, but I was in good spirits, knowing I had only a short ride ahead of me today.

I pushed hard down the road, passing golden fields filled with flowers. It was a scenic ride until I reached the outskirts of Vanadzor, an industrial city littered with factories, many of which had been shut down. The place was now the colour of rust.

At the Argishti Hotel just outside the city centre I asked for a room but the price seemed high so I rode on in search of a better option. Before I had got very far, a large pot-bellied man waved me over to his shop.

He wanted to hear all about what I was doing, and asked where I was staying. When he heard about the room price at the Argishti he picked up the phone, called the hotel and made a booking, pretending it was for himself – he got it for 20 dollars less.

The man at the front desk of the hotel was very understanding about having a bike parked in the grounds and acted like it happened all the time. On Tigran Mets, a pleasant boulevard of shops and bakeries, I found a cafe and sat outside. A group of school kids paraded down the street hand in hand shouting slogans celebrating their freedom at the end of the school year. The adults looked at them bewildered, but the kids enjoyed the public display and the attention they were getting. The men at the cafe began to talk about me loudly. People in Armenia don't do anything alone. You'll never see someone reading a book, because it is a solitary sport. Everything has to be done at least in pairs. Being a solo cyclist was one of many things that made me an obvious and inevitable topic of conversation. It would have taken only a few words to have made those men like brothers; such is the way in Armenia.

* * *

A busload of American missionaries were also staying in my hotel. In the breakfast room they chattered loudly and nasally about local football teams and wrestling. Then their leader took out a book and began the daily reading about unselfishness and giving through faith.

Their whole presence there made no sense to me at all. They had arrived in the most God-fearing

79

Christian nation on earth. What Christianity was there to spread? For most people in Armenia, their faith is all they have, and a busload of these guys wasn't going to affirm anything. It was like nutritionists visiting Eskimo colonies trying to teach them the advantages of having fish in their diet. They should have tried their luck in nearby Iran or Saudi Arabia instead.

I had a cheese omelette and wonderful homemade apricot jam that I could have eaten by the spoonful, but I was in a rush to get on my bike and away from those people. Lone travellers don't like having to listen to obvious comments – 'Look, a church'; 'Oh, the ice is just as cold as back home' – it's one of the reasons we travel by ourselves. I clicked my pannier bags into place, checked my wheels and hopped on just as the missionaries came outside. 'Where you goin' with that thing, buddy?' one of the guys called out.

'Alaverdi!' I yelled, and sped off.

Beneath overcast skies I pedalled down a series of quiet roads and out of the city. At the turn-off to Alaverdi a surreal banner advertised a strip club and casino five kilometres down the route I was taking. As soon as I was out of Vanadzor the scenery changed dramatically. I was now climbing through a forest thick with trees. The roadside was punctuated with tombstones at regular intervals – it was clearly a dangerous road, the site of many car accidents, but drivers paid no heed to this and wove around me at full throttle, regardless. This carefree attitude confirmed to me how religious Armenia is: fully secure in their belief in an afterlife, Armenians are not worried about living close to the edge.

The small strip club was perched all by itself on the cliff side, lost in the forest with no cars or signs of life anywhere around it. It was the oddest sight. The road turned downhill and began running alongside a large gorge with a river flowing through it. It would take me all the way to Alaverdi.

The road flowed through the mountains and I was flying at breakneck speeds. I kept thinking that it couldn't dip any lower, but still it kept dropping, down and further down, in an endless descent. I began loudly singing 'This Land is Your Land' by Woody Guthrie until I swallowed a bug and switched to humming. It was a perfect ride, the sort cyclists dream about: navigating through sharp bends and releasing the brakes to allow the bike to run on its own without holding back.

I whizzed through several dimly lit tunnels and past the glamorous Tufenkian Hotel, which looked like it should have been in the French Riviera instead of the Caucasus. At a petrol station a group gathered round me and bought me a coffee from the vending machine. It was worse than Starbucks, but I was touched by the gesture.

Up on a ridge, the road briefly ran alongside some railway tracks and just as I got there a train came trundling down the line. A group of railway workers in an open cart spotted me and waved and hollered encouragingly. I waved back as the whistle blew in a moment Steinbeck would have been proud of.

Eventually I came to a small village. A couple of sweet old ladies were selling delicious blackberries and raspberries by the roadside and they invited me to sit with them and rest. 'We have to sell the fruit just to be able to buy bread,' one of them told me. 'There's no work here for anybody. *Kordz chiga, pogh chiga.*' There's no work, and no money. I heard that same phrase everywhere I went. It was repeated almost like a catchphrase; it seemed to follow me around, like a pop song that had just been released. As elsewhere in Armenia, the many factories in this area had shut their doors following the break-up of the Soviet Union in 1991. They had once manufactured all kinds of goods but were now stripped down to their shells. Like everywhere else outside Yerevan and a few small cities, the local economy was now almost entirely agricultural.

The one local industry I did stumble across, a few kilometres before Alaverdi, was tombstone-carving. The bare slabs of rock had looked so inviting for a rest in the stillness and quiet of a shady tree but suddenly seemed less appealing when I found out they were about to be inscribed with the names and dates of the deceased.

The only accommodation Alaverdi had to offer turned out to be in a converted kindergarten. I carried my bike up the steps to the entrance, glad the ride was over. The doors to all of the rooms were open, but the building was empty. I sat out on the balcony and waited for someone to turn up. Eventually the cleaner, Lusine, arrived. She looked surprised to see a guest, but happily showed me the rooms and called the owner to arrange a price. I chose the 'deluxe' room, which was like a small apartment with bookshelves, a piano and a private bathroom. I had my own balcony as well that looked down over the factory across the river, with its smashed windows and derelict frontage. Smoke was rising from the top of the mountainside, where a giant cross had also been erected.

Later I found out the hotel was a family-run operation, and that Lusine was the Cinderella daughter-in-law to an otherwise awful family. The grandmother saw me as a giant dollar sign and tried to act nice while charging me an outrageous price for a meal. Her grandson, Lusine's husband, was a large, lazy man who slouched on the couch all day. I felt bad for the sweet girl stuck in the middle of it all.

I took a freezing cold shower, dipping a plastic ladle into a bucket of water to douse myself clean. Having spent time in India, I was used to this system of washing since it was the only available option almost everywhere I stayed while in the country. At the end of my month-long trip, I checked into the four-star Ambassador Hotel in Mumbai for a bit of comfort when I was feeling ill, and saw my first western shower in four weeks. It had a beautiful marble floor and high-end showerhead. But in a corner was still that small cheap plastic bucket, for Indian guests that weren't use to modern showers.

Feeling clean and refreshed, though shivering slightly, I went for a walk. Around the corner from my hotel, a group of ten older men sat under a tree playing cards and backgammon. 'Real Madrid or Barcelona?' one of them asked me. 'Barcelona,' I replied, which got me a round of cheers and a seat at their table with only one grumpy man sneering at my preference. They asked what on earth I was doing in Alaverdi. They also asked about my marital status, and quickly, in unison, agreed to find me a wife during my stay here. 'Armenian women are good women and they'll look after you,' one of them explained. I asked if they knew a girl who could ride a bicycle; I was awfully tired, I said, and maybe they knew someone that could ride the rest of the way while I sat on the back.

I walked across the bridge and alongside the walls

of the abandoned factory until I arrived at the cable car that would take me up the mountain to the tenth-century monastery of Sanahin. For the price of about ten pence, the tired-looking Soviet cable car, with its antiquated buttons and dials, creaked and groaned its way up the steep incline. An isolated village also named Sanahin sat on top of the ridge, affording a magnificent view of the gorge below. I walked through the streets admiring the small homes and impressive gardens full of fruit trees and frantic chickens, and then continued on up to the monastery. It was a very hot day and I arrived covered in sweat. The monks really liked having a view back in the day, I thought. Most Armenian churches and monasteries are located at high vantage points, not just to take in the scenery but for protection from invaders who enjoyed a good pillage and usually aimed to convert or kill the Christians within the walls. Personally I don't believe anybody has ever really killed anyone for their religious differences; there are usually much darker forces at play.

Sanahin Monastery was a breathtaking sight. Its large pillars were etched with crosses and there were carefully carved *khachkars* all around. Sunlight cascaded through the windows and illuminated the rooms; in the hallways elderly women lit thin yellow candles and prayed. As the women began to sing, I spotted a priest. He was an ogre of a man who must have owned a car – he clearly never walked any part of the hill up to the monastery. I was reminded of a funny story I heard once about an American who was sent to prison in North Korea. His crime? He was standing in the main square in Pyongyang in front of a lifelike statue

84

of Kim Jong-Il when two guards overheard him say, 'How come he's so fat and everybody else is so skinny?'

The grounds were beautiful, and an ancient cemetery added to the medieval atmosphere. On my walk back down to the cable car, I saw three women high up on a ladder wrestling with a cherry tree. They stopped me and insisted that I take a two-meter long branch full of bright yellow cherries. I was really touched but felt a little silly holding it as I walked down the road. The cherries were at a perfect stage of ripeness; they were the best I'd ever tasted. I left a trail of pips behind me.

Back down in Alaverdi I re-joined the old men. Their version of backgammon was different from the one I knew and my knowledge of cards didn't extend much beyond poker, so I chose to just watch. They played for sticks; the person who ran out of sticks first was the loser and had to buy everyone ice cream. The man named Ago rolled the dice and shouted that he was a professional backgammon player. 'Look how rich I am,' he said, showing his pile of sticks. 'I only ever eat ice cream.' Ago was known to everyone as 'the Greek', since his family had settled here from Greece a generation earlier. A nice man named Garen ordered some ice cream and a cold beer for me and asked a young boy to go fetch them. He seemed more refined than the others and told me he had been a *kyughabed* (village mayor) for many years. He wanted everyone to make a good impression and tried to make Ago tone down his jokes after he asked how much money I had and if I'd give him all of it. One of the men at the table – Hovig – was described as a driver. I took my chances and arranged to have him take me round the various monasteries in the area the following day.

Returning to my hotel, I looked at the shelf of books in my room and wished my Armenian reading skills were more advanced than those of a five-year-old. I then glanced at the piano and wished I knew how to play it. Finally I looked at the bed and remembered how good I was at sleeping.

Chapter 12

There's A Nice Girl You Should Meet

At breakfast the grandmother looked at me with distrusting eyes as she tried to crack a rare smile. I understood her resentment. There's a widely held belief that all Armenians outside of Armenia live like kings, and bitterness can fester among those who have led difficult lives. This isn't everyone's point of view, but some are really convinced of it, as though we members of the diaspora have the ability to rescue them but probably won't. There I was, in her eyes a giant cash cow, sitting in her dining room eating her stale bread, eggs, jam and cheese. Her dim grandson sat watching TV as she asked about my dinner plans. I said I was busy in the evening, and she sneered a little.

Hovig took me by surprise with his punctuality. We stopped to get some fuel for his black sedan and he opened the boot to get at the two large red metal canisters where the petrol would be stored. We walked away from the car during the fill-up, as the rule goes – one of the few actually followed in Armenia. Old Russian cars have been known to catch fire, although this could be due to the fact that the man filling it with fuel is usually smoking a cigarette. Seatbelts were also a new requirement in the country and I noticed Hovig's was broken. He solved the problem by wrapping his around the handbrake, as we sped up the steep pass. I had broken my fat taxi driver rule with Hovig, and it was a judgement call I didn't regret. He said he was fifty-eight but with his big belly and youthful eyes he looked like he was in his early forties. He was curious about England and the quality of life there, and offered, as seemed customary, to find me a wife.

After climbing a steep hill and rolling past some fields, we arrived at the ancient church of Odzun. The large gardens surrounding the church had an abundance of *khachkars*; inside, the pillared structure was littered with religious artefacts. Slabs of biblical rock carvings lay on the floor, resting against the walls, with no space to house them anywhere. The priest spoke excellent English and entertained some tourists with stories about the church. He said it was thought that Thomas the Apostle, one of Jesus's disciples, came to Odzun in the first century and buried Jesus's clothes under the altar, before going to India. He also talked about a stone brought from Jerusalem that was believed to be the very first depiction of the Virgin with the baby Jesus. He then launched into '*Der Voghormya*', an Armenian prayer song, to show off the church's great acoustics. I stood at the back as his voice resonated all around.

Hovig came over to me and whispered that there was a nice girl at the front of the church that I should meet. He began listing her good features. 'She's thirty, well educated in Yerevan, and from a good family I know well,' he proclaimed, excited by the prospect of playing matchmaker. We had a church, a priest and a small crowd, so I said we should just get it over with and have the ceremony there and then. He laughed sensing my sarcasm. To be honest, she wasn't much of a looker, and this was hardly the place to pick up chicks.

Back in the car, Hovig told me stories about all the different tourists he'd driven around over the years.

He was content with life. He had put his children through school, was able to look after his grandkids, and didn't need any more than that. He liked to do business honestly, he said, and found he actually earned more because of that. Recently he'd driven some Germans around and had refused the extra tip they offered, but the more he refused the more they gave him. He laughed.

Our next destination was the monastery of Akhtala, situated once again on a high cliff overlooking the gorge below. The old fortress walls surrounding the thousand-year-old monastery were still standing; with its defensive position and large metal gate the place looked like an old Scottish castle. Hovig pointed to a new monument that had been built in honour of marriage. The two 1.5-metre-high intertwined wedding rings seemed pretty fitting since I had nearly been married off twenty minutes earlier. Hovig said I should take a picture for good luck, and I posed in front, shrugging my shoulders and feeling like an ass.

The mossy exterior and haphazard angular roofs made me think Akhtala was a lot less grand than Odzun, but inside it was an entirely different story. The church interior was the most magnificent I had seen anywhere in the world. All around were frescoes in blue and gold depicting biblical stories painted a thousand years ago. The giant five-metre-tall representation of God, behind the altar, had been vandalized by previous conquerors and no longer had a face, but the rest of the pictures on the walls and ceiling were wonderfully intact and seemed to have aged exceptionally well. Hovig said Catholics had been involved with the construction of Akhtala, which was why it didn't get many visitors, because it wasn't purely

Armenian. I wandered around the church taking photographs until an angry woman disciplined me for stepping on a holy rug. I wondered if anyone was allowed to hoover it. Even the Pope has to have a shower and wash behind the ears once in a while. It strengthened how much I detest the sanctifying of objects.

Our last monastery was Haghpat. Hovig was born in that village and his sister also owned a small shop there. She had lost her husband in the Karabagh war nearly twenty years earlier, Hovig said, and had seen difficult days. To lighten the mood, he told me that the newly appointed priest in Haghpat had been transferred there from an Armenian church in Las Vegas. I found this disparity to be one of the funniest things I had heard in a long while and we both sniggered.

Haghpat is a tenth-century medieval Armenian monastery of white stone but over the years has come to look like someone has rubbed charcoal all over it. It is regarded as an architectural marvel because it's built into the hillside. Part of the structure lies below the green slope behind it; above ground, its multiple roofs and triangular pediments are stacked at different angles around the central orange-tiled dome. In the Middle Ages the complex served as a school and it has stood proudly intact ever since, withstanding earthquakes that have felled many other churches. The actual Sayat Nova stayed here when poverty brought his extensive travels to an end and he had no option but to become a monk. I tried to imagine his life there as I strolled around the buildings and stared down at the misty valley below. Inside one of the church's dark rooms, another priest began to sing '*Der Voghormya*' for some

American tourists, perhaps trying to rally up a tip with his tenor voice.

Hovig's sister was expecting us. She led me round to the small garden by the side of her shop, then hurried off to make coffee. Hovig began identifying the different trees, which his father had planted long ago. It was peaceful sitting under the fruit trees with the gorge far below us and those ever-present puffs of smoke rising from the mountain in the distance.

* * *

There's a restaurant in the region of Alaverdi that everyone visits when they come to town – Armen's. It's like Rick's Cafe in Casablanca in that respect. I had heard about Armen before I'd arrived. Some years ago he'd won a national *khorovadz* competition and every year since has been invited back as a judge. In a country where barbecues are a big deal, this was a tremendous honour.

There was no sign outside his restaurant, but I figured it had to be the place since there was nothing else around. I peered round the door and saw that a large wedding party was under way inside. Someone offered to take me to Armen. He was charismatic and I liked him immediately. I told him about my travels and how I didn't want to pass through the region without tasting his food. He found me a place to sit away from the party and soon plate after plate began arriving in front of me. There were salads of cucumber and tomatoes, cheeses of cow and goat, eggplant fried to a mouthwatering softness, and pork *khorovadz* that looked and smelled like a dream. Each dish was cooked to perfection, the work of a master chef, and I ate every last piece. Armen also threw in some complimentary vodka, lining up all the different varieties he had. The apple vodka was quite nice, but the pear left a twinge of aftertaste in my mouth for a good half hour. To finish, there was ice cream and coffee. It was a grand feast of the highest order and I went to the kitchen to thank everyone. They charged me half what the old woman back at the hotel had wanted for a bit of chicken.

As I was leaving, the wedding party was kicking off and the music was blaring. I figured all I had to do was say hello to someone and my evening would be full of new friends and dancing. But I also knew it would involve more alcohol and being force-fed. I couldn't eat another bite, not even a mint if it was wafer-thin. I quietly slipped out, conscious of the fact I was possibly missing the chance of a momentous evening. It was raining heavily now and water cascaded down the sides of the gorge, creating waterfalls everywhere. My stomach churned into a big happy smile.

Chapter 13

An Intoxicating Ride To Dilijan

Next morning I was back in Hovig's taxi again, this time with Sayat Nova secured to the roof rack. I had enjoyed the grand downhill on the way to Alaverdi, but it would have been a vicious test to reverse it all the way back up to Vanadzor. I wasn't intimidated by the uphill as much as the tunnels. Nobody likes to go backwards on the same road, but those unlit spaces were scary enough at racing speeds; struggling up them with no speed would have been much worse. There was another option, albeit an even more dangerous one: to use the road south via Noyemberyan, but it had been rated as highly risky due to the border conflicts with Azerbaijan.

Hovig and I discussed and solved many of life's problems during our drive. We passed some Iranians on the road. 'They come to Armenia to drink, run around with women, and do everything else they would be killed for doing in their own country,' he said in the manner of an experienced tour guide. We said our goodbyes in Vanadzor with a manly handshake. Hovig said to call if I was ever in Alaverdi again, or if I got in any trouble on the road on my trip. 'I'll be there in an hour wherever you are to help you,' he said, and I knew he meant it.

The streets were quiet as I pedalled out of Vanadzor, heading forever upwards. Just as I'd turn a bend and think the climb was over, a new twist took me further up. The sun was shining but distant clouds were brewing in darkness. Outside the city limits I stopped at a small shop for my daily supplies and to top up my water. An old farmer with a weathered face and no teeth came over to find out what I was up to. He introduced himself as Ohan, looked my bike up and down and, as others had done before him, asked why I was doing such a ridiculous thing. He didn't grasp the concept, and I didn't blame him. But he still wanted to be kind to a stranger. Pointing down the road he said his village, Margahovit, was thirty kilometres away. If I were to get there that evening, he'd give me a place to stay. I was non-committal in my reply, having learned long ago never to give definite promises unless I was a hundred per cent certain. You can easily hurt or insult people here that way.

The road continued to lead me up into the green hills. Clouds began to gather and the weather was cooling down. I pulled over to put on a jacket and a car stopped twenty metres behind me. The driver got out and made a coffee signal. I gave him a thumbs up and followed him into the nearby turn-off to a restaurant. It turned out he ran the place with his sisters: his name was Artur and he showed me around while the coffee was being prepared. It occupied a nice position on a slope that dropped down to the river and there were little coves for diners. He and his sixty-seven-year-old father had built the whole thing themselves.

'Eat! Drink!' his sisters instructed, and they began offering coffee, blackberry juice, profiteroles, *confets*, apricots… I obeyed enthusiastically. I was subjected to the usual line of questioning about my trip and marital status. Artur said he knew a lovely girl that was visiting nearby and that I should marry her. He said it in the way he might have told me to go down to the shop and buy some cheese. Without asking, he picked up his phone and began to see if he could locate her. His phone wasn't getting any reception and he couldn't get a signal. Damn technology and bloody rubbish satellites keeping me from meeting the wife, I thought. But he didn't stop there. Turning to his sister Ruzanna, a lovely plump lady, he asked, 'How old's your daughter now?' Ruzanna laughed a little and said, 'Too young.'

Back on the bike my legs were tired and the clouds grew thick and grumbled ominously around me. Just in time, I spotted a small picnic site on the side of the road with a barbecue pit, a table and a roof. Almost immediately as I'd taken cover, it began to rain. The drizzle quickly turned into a heavy downpour. The climb had left me covered in sweat and I began to feel cold even after I'd put on my raincoat as my final layer. I huddled in the corner of the tiny shelter, swinging my legs to keep warm, waiting for the weather to improve. The clouds were moving sluggishly, but at least I was dry. I watched the cars and large buses racing past, all of which had a good stare at Sayat Nova and me, looking slightly baffled. A caterpillar made its way towards my shoes. Wherever I moved, it followed. I admired its bravery.

After two hours the rain eased and I decided to push on. A couple of old ladies carrying very large sacks of tea yelled across at me, asking what I was doing out in this weather. They cackled with laughter and diagnosed me as crazy as I struggled on up the road. The skies filled with dark clouds once again, lightning flashed in the distance and thunder echoed through the mountains. The heavens opened and it began to pour viciously. I could barely see ahead of me: I had to take off my sunglasses, which I wore to protect my eyes from debris. I passed a few turn-offs to some villages, one of which was Margahovit, as I thought of the farmer's invitation earlier. I wanted to get off the road and take shelter but the dirt track leading towards the village was slowly turning into a muddy river. The rain turned to hailstones and all I could hear was the crashing of ice pellets against my helmet. Just when it felt like I was being pelted with golf balls, I spotted a petrol station up ahead, like a great mirage through the frozen rain. It even had a covered rest area. I sprinted the bike over and gave silent thanks. Buying things that advertise to be waterproof doesn't mean a thing in weather like this and I was soaked through to my very bones.

A young guy popped his head out of the petrol station and waved for me to come over. That's how I met Berj and Mesrob, who were running the place. They were about to sit down to lunch. Plates of dumpling stew, lamb, potatoes, tomatoes, cucumber and cheese lay before me as if they had been expecting me. I thanked them for rescuing me, took off my soaked clothes and got stuck in.

They were eager to learn about life in England and fired question after question at me as I tried to chew my food. They talked about how much they would have to pay in bribes just to get a visa to visit. Berj was more the dreamer and was excited at the mere thought of a trip to England, but Mesrob being the realist put him in his place, bringing up all the potential problems.

Berj presented a bottle of vodka and I thought, why not? Just a little to warm up the soul after the day's ride so far. 'Don't worry, you can sleep here tonight if the weather stays like this,' he said, and we toasted our meeting.

After each glass I would say that was the last one, and he'd agree. This went on for half an hour until we'd finished off the bottle between the two of us while Mesrob sat and watched. We had coffee dark as night and continued feasting on what remained on the table. They mentioned a nice girl who worked with them sometimes and said she would make a good match for me. Sadly she wasn't on shift that day. The conversation moved back to England and they began to go through everything I owned, asking what the price of it was. '*Tang eh, eli!*' they'd exclaim, in shock at how expensive everything was. I tried to explain that sure we made money in the West, but life was so expensive that everyone lived in debt.

Berj began to call his friends from the nearby village to come by and meet me. They slowly arrived one by one, including the village mayor, who wore a bright red hat to stand out and acted more like a tough guy than the others. A lanky fellow named Mher was really excited by the bike and asked if he could take it for a ride. We all ventured outside in the rain to watch Mher make circles around the station. Everyone laughed their heads off and took pictures on their phones. We had turned into a fun bunch and I was feeling rather jolly. Berj and Mesrob kept running in and out to serve customers that were coming by. I was preparing to spend the night there when Berj burst back through the door and exclaimed, 'The sun is out and you can continue your ride!' Looking at my map, I saw that it was a twenty-kilometre downhill through the mountains to get to Dilijan. I decided to take my chances.

Now, I can't tell you exactly what happened next

97

because to be honest I don't remember most of it. I waved goodbye to my new friends and the alcohol hit me hard with my first breath on the descent. This was a bad idea. I remember singing a lot as I tried to hold my bike straight and navigate downhill. All that fresh air I *should* have enjoyed only made me more intoxicated. I swerved through the curves of the road, pressing my disc brakes to their limit. I had been against getting disc brakes before the journey because they make a bike heavy, but they were worth their weight here. I remember meeting some old farmers who happened to be even drunker then I was. One of them was named Raffi like me. They encouraged me on, shouting and screaming. Through the blank void in my memory and out the other side, I arrived in Dilijan's town centre in the early evening.

I saw a monstrously large lady on the street and asked where I might find a hotel. She called over a construction worker to show me the way and after a sobering walk up a steep hill we arrived at the place – a few cottages behind a gate – but nobody was home. Some neighbours got involved in my predicament. They called up the owner, who happened to be away, and warned me that the guard dog behind the gate was vicious. Then they phoned another friend who rented out rooms. But I ended up back down the hill at the gargantuan lady again. This time she pointed me in the opposite direction, down a hundred steps, which was hard work with the bike after the day I'd had. I sat and waited on a bench surrounded by flowers and played with a puppy for a while. Eventually a frail, kindly old man arrived. His wife was away, and it was obvious she was the brains behind the hotel operation, but he showed me to a room with a kitchen and a large bed for US $5. (Armenians don't trust their own currency and prefer to have their savings in money that has a better chance of keeping its value.) I was exhausted mentally and physically and could do nothing more than strip off my wet clothes, put my head down and fall into a deep sleep.

* * *

I needed warm water and a place to dry everything out. I wanted to feel human again. The bathroom where I was staying had a toilet you needed a PhD in quantum physics and a master's in engineering to be able to flush. The sink tap had no left or right to even pretend there was hot water, it only went straight up. The bar of soap looked like it had last been used back in the 90s then left to rot. By that I mean the 1890s. I have a travel rule that when things look bleak and your attitude is in danger of turning negative, you have to change the mood by doing nothing and finding some comforts. Today was going to be a rest day.

Nestled in the forests of Dilijan National Park, Dilijan is traditionally a spa town, known for its beauty and tranquillity. It's sometimes described as Armenia's Switzerland but I don't think that statement was conjured up by anyone that's actually been to Switzerland. Still, its densely wooded landscape is invigorating, and for centuries artists and the affluent used to retreat here, in search of inspiration and rehabilitation. Now it's a place for barbeques and weekend getaways for people from the capital.

In the early morning, Sayat Nova and I made our way to the Old Dilijan Tufenkian Hotel. I had passed the hotel the night before on my ride into town but thought it would be too extravagant. Today I didn't care. The design of the hotel attempted to re-create the ambience of a traditional village. Tourists were arriving by the busload to walk around the bread shop and ceramics shop, and to see woodcarvers dressed in old-fashioned garb showing off their handiwork. Sure, it was incredibly cheesy, but it was done in the most tasteful way possible. The wooden cabins were dotted around the mountainside and had carefully decorated modern rooms inside. Despite repeated requests, nobody came to collect my laundry, so I laid out everything I had on the floor, spreading it into every corner of the room, and watched the opening stage of the Tour De France in my birthday suit. I wondered how fat Sayat Nova would feel, with his heavy pannier bags and robust frame, compared to those seven-kilogramme racing bikes. I was glad he wasn't there with me; instead, he was resting in the storage room next to the caretaker's office.

As I put my head down for a mid-morning nap, about twenty buses pulled up and blocked the whole road. A dance competition for kids was being held at the Greek-style amphitheatre nearby. The entire assemblage of two hundred people decided to camp outside my door and fix their girls' hair while yelling out instructions as loudly as possible. I could hear Armenian music blaring in the distance and someone on a microphone that loved the sound of his own voice. It looked like there'd be no rest for me today. But an hour later a heavy downpour cancelled the event and the crowd dispersed in a mad dash. A wicked smile spread across my face.

Chapter 14

House of Tatoul

I woke up in a comfy bed with mounds of soft pillows and wondered when I'd be this comfortable again. The sky was overcast and the clouds hung in place without a breeze or whisper to scurry them along, but it was not raining. Outside my door was a pack of twenty dogs waiting to pick a fight. They trotted up the street with organized aggression. Perhaps they'd heard there was a bicycle nearby.

The weather was good enough to ride and I decided to head towards Parz Lich ('Simple Lake'), which came recommended by a friend. I gathered up all my wet, dirty clothes from the floor and collected my bike from the kind caretaker who proudly presented it as if he'd been guarding it day and night.

On the road, I had to keep asking for directions. Everybody told me to just go straight, even though the road kept splitting into a Y every few minutes. So I'd stop and pull over and repeat my routine until eventually I found the turn-off towards the lake.

The road, if you could call it that, was a continuous minefield of cracks and scattered rocks; it looked impossible to cycle on. I had changed my tyres to slicks specifically for my Armenia tour and the loose gravel and potholes of the lake road would have shredded them to pieces if I'd attempted to ride. So I walked. For most of the way the track wound steeply up through the mountains, serenely shaded by trees and full of the quiet whispers of nature. I saw a car only once every half hour and was met with stupefied looks.

Part way up I reached a hotel with a beautiful cobblestone path leading up into the mountain. The building was still under construction, but according to Felix, one of the workmen on the site, would be finished in a month, which was hard to believe. Felix and I got chatting. He told me that he had fought in the Karabagh War from start to end – all six years of it, from 1988 to 1994 – but had got nothing from the Armenian government for it. People had asked him why he'd even fought. 'What are you going to do?' he sighed. 'That's our land and our people.'

Surrounded by deep forest, with rich vegetation all around me, I began to wonder whether I would ever emerge from the woods. But as the road started to descend I heard Armenian music in the distance and knew I was close. I swiftly made my way along the final gravel curves and down to a pass through the trees. There before me was the lake. Actually, it was more like a rather large puddle.

A group of teenagers were dancing to Armenian music and Russian pop at the restaurant complex next to the lake. The owners looked at me with distrustful eyes. 'Why didn't you bring a girl with you?' one of them asked with genuine concern. I explained how I wasn't any good at riding a tandem. I ordered a beer and sat outside on a bench as a disgruntled employee brought it out to me. Lanky, bespectacled and with a cigarette hanging from his lips, he looked the very definition of disappointment. It was a sweet beer I could barely stomach, but I enjoyed sitting among the trees in the late afternoon.

My room was a small wooden shack with two single beds. It smelled quite new with the fire retardant still sticking to everything. The smell triggered powerful memories of childhood summers at Camp Nubar in upstate New York where Armenian kids gather every year. I went on to become a counsellor at the camp when I was nineteen. The smell took me back to happy times by the majestic Lake Arax, young summer love, and rolling around the green grass of the football pitch at night, locked with tender lips. It was probably the most memories anyone's ever got from the chemicals of fireproof lacquer without purposely sniffing it.

Some workers were building more cabins next to mine and were hard at work cutting wood and nailing everything in place. I tried to put my head down for a siesta, but the Russian techno and saw-cutter weren't a good recipe for sleep. I went for a walk around the lake. Ducks waddled in the shafts of sunlight that glistened through the trees. A gentle breeze blew and it was all quite serene, even if the lake was so small it couldn't drown a fish.

I watched as youngsters escaped from their parties, away from parental supervision, and went running off in packs. One kid who couldn't have been more than twelve walked as if he was a forty-year-old man, with a real tough-guy manner about him. He ordered his friends around with stern instructions and yelled out when he didn't get his way.

I spent part of the afternoon going over my bike, tightening things and assessing how everything was running. I gave Sayat Nova a good rubdown and cleaned the build-up of dirt. An old dog eyed me warily as he circled the grounds. He looked very sickly but was clearly determined to show that this was his territory.

I soon found myself sitting with the three guys who

were building the cabins next to mine. Eighteen-year-old Ohan wasn't interested in the work and came over to ask about all the parts on my bike. He was tired of the smell of lacquer and working without a mask and was very open about how much he didn't want to do anything. In his restlessness he began to spray-paint his phone-cover white and started calling it an iPhone. We moved on to discussing life in England and the beauty of Armenia. He repeatedly asked questions about England and mentioned how much he'd like to visit. I told him he'd go and come straight back when he started missing the lake, and he laughed ferociously at the thought. He was off to the army in four months but didn't seem worried.

His workmate Artur was older and more sanguine. He ordered some coffee and asked if I'd like to join him collecting crayfish from the lake a bit later. The sun was slowly setting behind the mountains as we boarded a small rowboat. Artur let me row, and I was quite excited to do so, although I kept that fact to myself. To him, this was work. I rowed to the Styrofoam pieces sticking out of the water and Artur pulled up the cages and hoisted the crayfish into a bucket. They were dark and brown from the muddy earth and didn't look like much. Disappointed, Artur said he would have thrown these back in Lake Sevan, which was near where he lived. We moved on to the next set of Styrofoam floats. I tried to row as expertly as possible, not to look like an incompetent foreigner. Artur pulled up more cages full of old *khorovadz* bones and stinky fish being used as bait. Some came up empty; others contained a handful of sad-looking crustaceans. We returned to shore with a full bucket and dumped our catch into a large fish tank. Artur

104

threw in a dead fish and we watched as the crayfish attacked it.

I was feeling rather hungry myself as I entered the restaurant for dinner. I sat down to chicken *khorovadz*, potatoes, cheese and delicious homemade bread. Anahit was the boss of the kitchen and nobody walking in could have doubted that. She was a tough lady with an Inca-gold smile and she ran the kitchen with a cigarette hanging from her lips, pouring shots of vodka for herself periodically while swearing like a sailor. Part way through my meal, the power failed and everything went dark, but the bad Russian pop on the stereo still kept playing. It was as though the back-up generator had been put there just for that eventuality.

After dinner I sat in the restaurant with the workforce, pouring shots of vodka and exchanging stories. (Still no joy with the pear vodka, whose aftertaste seemed to last a lifetime.) The boys teased Chef Anahit about her solitary drinking and tried to get her to pour us a few extra shots so we could all join in together. She complained of tiredness and said she was waiting for her ride home. I offered her a lift on my bike, but to no avail. Artur did manage to winkle a few potatoes out of her, and some extraordinarily large gherkins, and we set off to build a fire outside. As we watched the flames, Ohan would periodically let his impatience get the better of him, nibbling at a series of undercooked potatoes. Eventually they were ready and we pulled them out of the fire with sticks. We sat in the moonlight as the fire grew dim and the stars shone brighter and ate the potatoes just as they were.

* * *

It's always a little disheartening to backtrack, especially when the terrain is not at all bike-friendly. So when a car pulled up behind me, about halfway back along my return route to Dilijan, I did not hesitate to accept a lift for Sayat Nova and myself. The man in the driving seat was Kevork, who seemed to be the owner of the Parz Lich resort where I'd been staying. As we continued on to Dilijan, Kevork told me how the previous year he had accidentally hit two cows on that road with his car. He complained about the damage it had caused to his vehicle and how much it had cost to get the windscreen replaced, never once mentioning the story from the perspective of the cow. I knew whose side I was on.

As we pulled into Dilijan a young taxi driver named Tatoul approached and said he knew a place I could stay. He pointed in the direction I'd be heading the next morning – towards Lake Sevan – and I took that as a good sign. He duly escorted Sayat Nova and me up the road to a little house overlooking the forest below. Tatoul began to give me a tour of the place, opening every door and cupboard to show where everything was. It all looked as though it had been left idle for far too long, with a thick layer of dust carpeting everything. What sold it for me was the large balcony with a clothesline where I could finally do my laundry and dry out my clothes.

Tatoul eventually left me, having gone through all the locks and cupboards a second time. I took a walk back into town to find some much needed laundry detergent. The stony-faced woman in the shop said she only had rose-scented detergent. I told her that was perfect and that I liked to smell pretty. I spent the next ten minutes doing my best stand-up material but I didn't even get a smirk out of her. Back at the house I devoted a good hour to washing my clothes in the bathtub. There was no hot water (a detail Tatoul failed to mention during his tour) and I worked hard twisting and squeezing all the dirt out. You only know how dirty your clothes actually are when you hand-wash them. The water immediately turned an ugly brown. I drained the tub, added fresh water, and repeated the process over and over again until I was satisfied with the colour of the water. I hung my clothes up outside, fighting small spiders for space along the line. As I placed my last peg on my final rose-scented T-shirt, it began to rain. I just left everything hanging. I was too tired and disheartened to do anything else.

Inside, the TV produced a half picture and then made the most unearthly noise. I was sure it was about to burst as I quickly turned it off and a smoky smell filled the room. I went to the bedroom and put my head down, even though it was still bright outside. As I did so, the house shook violently and I wondered if a small earthquake had hit. It turned out to be the cars passing by outside. Wave after wave of traffic sent tremors through the house and my body shivered from the cold of the broken window.

I recalled having been in only one place worse than this. I was in India and had just arrived at the 'holy' city of Varanasi. Exhausted after a sixteen-hour train journey, I trudged out of the station and checked into the first hotel I could find. I threw my bags down, put some biscuits I had just bought on a table, and collapsed on the bed. After a few minutes I heard a rustling sound and looked up to see that a mouse had climbed on to the table and was eating my biscuits. I grabbed everything, went down to reception and asked nicely for a new room. The receptionist was a sulky sort of man and seemed greatly annoyed.

'What's wrong with the room?' he barked

'There's a mouse in it.'

At this point he could have said any number of things, but his response was, 'How big is the mouse?' Perhaps they had a chart that specified what sized mouse was deemed acceptable by the management.

I was baffled by his reply and countered with, 'Why, do you know him?'

Eventually he gave in and sent someone to show me my new room. An overexcited little man carried my bags, opened the door to my new accommodation and with a big smile said, 'Everything okay, sir?'

I looked up with a sense of dread and said, 'What is that?' (I actually swore in that sentence.) Hanging over the bed was a giant member of the lizard family, a good metre and a half long.

The little Indian man didn't hesitate for a second. 'No problem, sir,' he said. And again, 'No problem, sir.' He raced out and returned with a broom, then proceeded to chase the lizard for a good ten minutes until he had shooed it out the window. Covered in sweat, he stood next to me and once again with a big smile asked, 'Everything okay, sir?', extending his hand for a tip for his efforts.

I continued to shake as the sound of rain pattered outside my window and my dream of clean, dry clothes began to diminish. I couldn't sleep.

This gloomy house also came with its own mouse, and I named him Charlie.

Chapter 15

The Death-Wish Tunnel

The first glorious rays of sunshine appeared over the mountains, throwing luscious yellows through my window. I was so happy to see the sun. Steam was billowing off my garments on the washing line outside. It was a beautiful sight.

Tatoul arrived and I lied and told him everything was wonderful. I packed up and set off for Lake Sevan, knowing it was going to be a long day. My map showed a massive climb up the mountain but everyone I asked told me not to worry, that there was a tunnel.

I began in good spirits, stopping to say hello to the many corn sellers who had set up improvised stalls on the side of the road. It was a blistering hot day and one of the vendors stopped me and told me to rest. With his grey whiskers and farmer's hat, he could easily have passed for seventy, but he told me he was only fifty-eight. Life was tough there, he said. Everyone was poor. His son wanted to get married but couldn't afford a ring for his fiancé. He sold about ten corncobs a day – not even enough to buy bread. I wanted to make that eleven, but I couldn't stomach the idea of eating a corncob with the sun burning down on me.

Up and up I climbed, crisscrossing back and forth, longing for a view of the tunnel everyone kept going on about. The road was tight, with almost no shoulder, and a constant flow of traffic careered carelessly through the bends. Cars honked and passengers waved at me, entertained by my presence there. I kept a calm head and carried on, walking now and slathered in sweat, unable to ride the gradient. In Tour de France terms, this was the Col du Tourmalet and I didn't have a feather-light bike or the shaved legs to conquer it.

I had presumed with all of this tunnel talk that it would be located somewhere near the base of the mountain. Silly me. Only after three hours of trudging did I finally spot the tunnel in the distance, near the very top of this apparently never-ending climb. You'd think that during the construction process someone would have stood up and said, 'Hold on a minute… it's only ten metres to the top from here… Instead of burrowing through all this rock, we might as well just build a road over the mountain… eh?' (Presuming that person was Canadian and said 'eh?' after every sentence.)

Just in front of the entrance to the tunnel was a gang of about a hundred soldiers. I was wary of approaching them, not knowing why they were there. But when I pulled over and said hello, they all gathered around me excitedly, asking what I was up to.

'Take me with you,' one of them yelled, and took a seat on the rack.

'It would be much better if you were a beautiful woman,' I told him.

They turned out to be a really good bunch of young guys, bored to death with their military service. My presence provided a nice distraction from their daily tasks. They didn't seem to be subject to any obvious discipline or formalities. They were just kids looking for an escape and entertainment like every other teenager. I offered my bike to whoever wanted to go for a ride, and one by one they climbed on, whizzing down the road and back up again, as all the other soldiers broke into fits of giggles.

'Commander! Commander! Look, I'm cycling,' a young soldier screamed at an indifferent older man. One of the soldiers asked if I wanted to take a gun with me and showed me his piece. Another examined my bike helmet and said that their bullets would go straight through it, and that it was no good. Finally, after enough of them had had a turn, I could put it off no longer. It was time to tackle the tunnel.

Fifty metres from the dark entrance, a tunnel guard came running over and warned me to be extra careful. I entered the hollow of doom walking along the right-hand shoulder amidst a flickering stream of dim lights and a horrid smell of petrol. Cars came screaming past as I climbed over the large pipes that blocked my narrow path, like on an army boot-camp exercise, until there was no path at all. Nothing.

I stood and waited for the traffic to stop, and when it did I hopped on the bike and rode like a madman in a massive sprint, searching for the next bit of right-hand shoulder. I thought of the great sprinter Thor Hushovd as I hunched over my front handlebars, legs pumping hard until I reached the safety of the next curb. I repeated this several times over the two kilometres, all the while singing The Smiths' 'There Is A Light That Never Goes Out', desperate for a glimpse of that gleaming brightness at the other end. Finally, after more potholes, massive pipes and Green Jersey-deserving sprints, I made it out of the hellhole and started the lovely descent to glistening Lake Sevan below.

I reached civilization again near the statue of Akhtamar, on the northern shore of the lake. The statue refers to a famous legend and depicts a princess with her arms outstretched, holding up a light. The original princess lived on a small island in a place called Lake Van, once the centre of the Armenian Urartu kingdom, with beautiful Armenian monasteries lining its shores, but now located in Turkey. The princess, whose name was Tamar, fell in love with a commoner. He would swim over to her island home every night, guided by the light she held up for him. One day her father the king learned of this affair and smashed her light, causing the boy to lose direction in the middle of Lake Van. His last words before he drowned were '*Akh*… Tamar' (Oh… Tamar) and it is said that his voice can still be heard at night around the lake. Lake Sevan (Lake Black Van) is named after the original lake that is now in Turkish territory. *Sev* means 'black': although the lake shimmers blue when illuminated by the sun, it turns deep black when clouds hover over it.

The lake was looking pretty black when I reached it. The sky was thick with clouds and there was a blustery wind. I had planned to camp on the lakeshore, but the weather turned me off that idea. Instead I checked into a beautifully located lakeside hotel and chose a room with a grand view of the water. Kohar, the manager, invited me down for some beer and crayfish. To be honest, I didn't know how to peel the crayfish or what bits to eat, so I just tore it to pieces and hid everything that looked unappealing. What parts I *did* eat were rather tasty. Two other hotel employees came and sat with us and I spent a happy hour having the three large and lovely ladies smother me with attention. They asked about my trip, about England, and why I couldn't take Kohar home with me. Back in my room I relaxed and watched the Tour de France. Greipel put in a great sprint at the end and won the stage. It was a master class of speed and I couldn't help comparing it to my own efforts in the tunnel earlier.

During dinner I watched the clouds hover over Lake Sevan, like fingers slowly caressing the water's skin. Kohar brought me a large feast of delicious pork *khorovadz* with fried potatoes, salads, bread, cheese and complimentary vodka. I polished off the lot, replenishing the burnt calories of the day. Then a group of men invited me over to their table for a drink. Two of them, in their sixties, were already quite drunk; the other, in his thirties, seemed quite sober and serious. They poured me shots of vodka and forced me to eat some fish as they toasted my Armenian-ness (and anything else that came to mind). The drunkest and oldest man then excused himself, saying he had to drive to Alaverdi (a good 100 kilometres away) to see his lover. 'I'm sixty-three and I have a lover,' he slurred, surprised at where life had led him. Dear God, I have to share the road with these people I thought again, not for the first time. The other drunken man hurried out and came back with Kohar and another lady. He asked which one I wanted, or if I wanted both. He was being an idiot and Kohar's eyes filled with anger and embarrassment at his behaviour. Later he too got in his car and drove off. I wouldn't have trusted him to tie his own shoelaces in the state he was in.

* * *

Lake Sevan is the largest lake in Armenia, fed by twenty-eight rivers and streams. It is also one of the highest freshwater lakes in the world, standing at 1,900 metres above sea level. During the Soviet era, between the 1930s and 50s, a project was conceived to drain a section of the lake and construct a hydroelectric plant. It proved disastrous and the plant never materialised, but the geography of the lake was altered, not least at Sevanavank, which used to be an island but is now a peninsula.

Yerevantsis go to Sevanavank to party, whereas tourists treat it as a sort of pilgrimage because of its famous ninth-century monastery. Two churches – Surp Arakelots and Surp Astvatsatsin – stand alongside each other on a high ridge, affording scenic views of the lake below. But all you can hear is blaring music because large groups of partying weekenders make it the traveller's pit stop from hell. Ironically, the monastery has a history of dealing with revellers. In the 1800s it was used as a sort of rehab centre for naughty monks from the church of Etchmiadzin. They came here to practise abstinence – from meat, wine and little boys.

I had said goodbye to Kohar and friends earlier that morning. They seemed sad to see me go. Kohar asked me to stay with them for a month and to forget about all this cycling. She said I'd always have a place there if I stopped by again. Hordes of small flies attacked me on the short ride to Sevanavank. They crawled behind my sunglasses and I accidentally ate a few, counting them as my protein intake for the morning. Having found a small place to rent near the edge of the lake, I was quite content until 10 a.m. came around and the music started. It was a mixture of hip hop, Russian techno and Armenian pop, each of which would have been bad enough on its own. Blended together, it was unbearable. I immediately missed my friends on the quiet side of the lake.

As the day wore on, jet skis and powerboats zoomed around the water, playthings of the privileged few. Tough guys cranked up their car stereos and danced to the music in their underwear and gold chains. The tourist board would have been proud.

The engine roars, music and accompanying smell of barbequed meat took their toll and I decided to walk up the steep steps to the two churches. All along the path, salesmen were peddling items to fat Armenian-American tourists who had to stop to take a breath every other step. Very few items were crafted in Armenia and some were even made in Turkey, which came as a surprise. I entered the first church at the top, pausing to take in its orange roof tiles and black tuff walls, admiring the hand-carved stones and dimly lit hush. The flames of the small yellow candles inside were still and never seemed to waver. Sophisticated thirteenth-century *khachkars* lay strewn around outside, seemingly neglected. I wondered what the American visitors thought of this casual attitude to Armenia's rich heritage, knowing how much they prized their own historic artefacts, often no more than a hundred years young. I climbed higher to escape the crowds and get a better view of Lake Sevan. The sun shone beautifully across the water and I enjoyed a few moments of peace.

Chapter 16

Cash The Turk Slayer

With my head full of Tour de France flashbacks and my heart keen to escape the tourist ghetto, I readied Sayat Nova at sun-up and prepared for the eighty-kilometre ride to Martuni. I knew this would be one of the flattest stages of my trip and was looking forward to some fast riding. I pedalled away from Sevanavank, swallowed a few fruit flies, took the turn-off onto yet another massively over-engineered flyover, and headed on the road that led straight to Martuni.

The road dipped and rose back up continuously without much shoulder lane to ride on. Still, the tarmac was better than most of the surfaces to date and my tyres rolled along smoother than at any point on the trip so far. This all helped me climb the rises like a champ. The bike felt good and so did I, knowing there was conquerable terrain ahead with no massive ascents. Young children were herding sheep and cows in the fields to my right; to my left the blues of Lake Sevan glowed ever more brilliantly the higher the sun rose. I rode the first stage hard, my legs firing like two perfect pistons as I aggressively approached the small climbs. I coasted sweetly on the downhills, taking the time to enjoy the splendours around me. The gentle breeze made it perfect riding weather – just enough to cool me but not strong enough to slow me down.

At a Y in the road I pulled over, not sure which way to turn. A car had stopped up ahead and I approached it to ask for directions. The old man driving seemed to have a hard time digesting the sight of me in the middle of nowhere. He had the whole family crammed inside the car. As soon as I began to speak Armenian, he grew excited, jumped out of the car and started handing me apricots. He explained every bend in the road between there and Martuni. He loved that an Armenian would do a journey like this around the country. The whole family forced more apricots into my bags as they wished me well, and we all continued in the same direction. The children waved to me for as long as I remained within their sights.

At the halfway point, I stopped at the ancient wonder of Noratus. I was looking forward to seeing this place, and had set it up as part of my itinerary a long time ago. Noratus is a large field of more than nine hundred ancient *khachkars* dating back to the tenth century, when the tradition started. The field sat high above the village with a backdrop of high mountains all around. I immediately sensed the grandness of the setting. Some lovely kids approached me and asked, in English, if I wanted a tour. Their grandmother sat next to a stone nearby, knitting socks for tourists. Row after row of moss-covered *khachkars* spread out in front of me, each with its own unique cross design and message. One of the most prized was the wedding stone, depicting a marriage ceremony and subsequent celebrations. It had been carefully cleaned, to make the details more visible. The simple carvings showed a few round faces and half bodies, a plate here, a jug of wine there, and a crooked table with more curious-looking plates. Unusually, the carver had etched a frame around the scene and added decorative patterns along the edges.

I stopped to buy a drink from a sweet old lady and she invited me for coffee. Her granddaughter was knitting a beanie hat with an Armenian flag design. I pointed at the French and Italian ones outside the shop and asked if she had made them too. She smiled and said yes, the tourists liked them. The grandmother was refreshingly positive about Armenia. She said Noratus was a beautiful place and the village was very peaceful. I gazed at the surrounding hillsides as the wind blew softly. It really was. Just then the silence was broken by a loud car horn as three young men in an old Soviet truck drove by yelling, 'Watermelons! Watermelons!'

As I walked back to my bike, a couple of kids rolled up the hill on their bicycles. I complimented them on their wheels, especially the full-suspension one that said 'Rambo' on it. I really thought it was nifty and I encouraged them to keep cycling.

Back at the junction to Martuni, a woman was singing a sweet love song to the cows she was tending in the field. I headed down the steep incline with her voice still filling my ears. People were selling fish from the lake by the side of the road; some had shops, others simply dangled them off makeshift stalls. The scenery changed dramatically as I got closer to my destination. I still had the southern reaches of Lake Sevan within view but was now riding on a cliff overlooking the lake. It was like being on the Pacific Coast Highway in California with the blue water glowing in rich beams of light. It was the perfect backdrop with hardly a car on the road.

* * *

Martuni was a pretty uninspiring place, with just a few strips of road filled with shops and a barely noticeable square. But I decided to take a rest day here for my knees and backside. I found a room in a worn old Soviet building that had once been a glorious palace. Now it just said 'Hotel' on the outside and had a derelict lobby and a staircase strewn with construction equipment inside. I assumed it was out of commission but decided to explore just for fun. As I approached the third floor, I heard voices and came upon three fat ladies. They were a tough trio, but I lightened the mood and they warmed up quickly, offering me a nice place to store Sayat Nova for the night. The largest of the ladies, with an arse the size of an Oldsmobile, looked at the bike and said, 'Cycling makes you skinnier, right?' I said it did and told her she was welcome to go for a ride, but she shyly declined my offer.

My room had been newly redecorated and smelled of paint. The toilet paper was the tough stuff, like harsh-grade sandpaper, and I was glad I still had some of my own packed in my bag. In the Western world you usually judge a hotel by the softness of its towels; in Armenia it's the softness of the toilet paper.

I put my bags down and went for a beer in the billiards hall next door. It was a large dimly lit room like something out of the 1950s, with ten tables packed close together and a side room that said 'VIP' on it. Four kids were playing, but it wasn't pool and it sure wasn't snooker. They played with one dark ball and the rest were all white. The point of the game was to pocket eight white balls first, which didn't seem very challenging with such an open table.

Back at the hotel, I went for coffee with the

caretaker, Mano, who also doubled as the barman. There was a toughness about him. His white hair was slicked back and he was dressed all in black from his button-down shirt all the way to his shoes, making him look like an Armenian Johnny Cash. Although he swore in every sentence, it became apparent that he was actually incredibly kind. It was also clear that he was lonely in Martuni and longed for some adventure. He told me about his children, how he had got a doctor to write that his son had a medical condition that meant he was unfit for military service – the same method employed to get kids out of gym class when I was growing up. He talked about how important it was to educate them, and explained that they now lived in Germany where there was the chance for a better life.

He also filled me in on the history of the hotel. At one time the place was so popular that people used to queue up to eat there, but now hardly anyone came. He told me humorous tales of generous gangsters he had befriended, how he liked his ladies, and how many Turks he had killed. I didn't ask him if this had been during wartime or just in passing. He spoke of the importance of marrying an Armenian, and how it was too bad his daughter was already married. I liked Mano. We were glad to have each other's company amidst the derelict emptiness of the place.

Chapter 17

An Awakening On The Selim Pass

Many people had warned me about the Selim Pass, which reached 2,300 metres at its highest point. 'Once you get to the top, you'll just have to sit on your ass all the way down to Yeghegnadzor,' Mano had said the night before. He looked down at me from the hotel balcony as I set off and yelled out that I was going the wrong way. I pointed to my map, but he said it would be much quicker if I went in the opposite direction. God knows what the other bit of road was like: the stretch he directed me to was bad enough, full of loose gravel and potholes everywhere.

I'm glad I did take his advice, though, because I met the nicest people on that little bit of road via the village of Geghhovit. Everyone walking past me stopped to say hello and find out what I was up to. I asked one old woman if I was heading the right way and she yelled out as if she had been waiting years for someone to ask that question. 'Straight! Just straight! Don't you dare turn left or right, just straight!' She wished me well, she said, because I was Armenian.

I climbed through sleepy Geghhovit and crossed a small river that shimmered in the sun. The road only seemed to go up, but I had great views of the mountain ranges in the distance. Just after the village an old farmer walking down the road stopped to chat. He was carrying a one-litre Coke bottle full of water and insisted I fill my own bottle with it. He was wearing a dusty old hat and as he smiled I saw the one tooth he had left hanging proudly. I tried as hard as I could to resist taking his daily water ration, since I had plenty, but he wouldn't have it any other way. '*Sarne!*' (It's cold!), he yelled and forced it on me, insisting his water was superior. I thought of all the rich men I've known who wouldn't even give you a stick of gum. He shouted out his best wishes for my journey and carried on down the road, like a vision swept away in a brush of wind.

I continued the climb, crossing between two great mountain ranges before I got cow-blocked. A man was hollering at his cows, which had swarmed over the entire road, and then hollering at his young son to round up the strays. I couldn't get past so we started to talk, and soon I was helping position the cows in line with my bike, like a cycling cowboy. Eventually the road cleared and the man yelled out for me to have a safe journey. I headed on towards the sun; my tyres caked with a fresh layer of cow dung.

A while later I found myself suddenly surrounded by flowers. My view became a collage of yellows, purples, reds and blues. It was so serene that I wished I knew the names of each and every species, including the useless Latin ones. The only thing better than the scenery was that there were no cars on the road. My route continued to rise steeply and I began to sweat buckets through the tough gradient, feeling every last bit of the bike's weight, and my own. After about three hours I reached the pass and stared down at the large canyon below me with a sense of victory.

As I soaked up the panorama, I couldn't help feeling a love for the land stretching out before me. Some ancient part of me was reignited at the sight of it. This soil, this greenery, the vastness of these mountains, they were all a part of what made me. Who

I am was born in this soil; my identity would always be from here, wherever in the world I laid my head. This was something I never truly understood until that moment. I remembered how my parents used to scold me to speak in Armenian when I was growing up, even though English tripped more naturally off my tongue. I thought now how grateful I should be to be a part of something bigger than myself, a culture rich in history and tradition, and the luck and determination of survival.

I couldn't have cared less about it when I was young, too distant to fathom, too removed to understand. As a kid at the Armenian school in Los Angeles I attended, I was so underwhelmed by the legend of Vartan Mamikonian, the fifth-century hero who ensured the survival of the Armenians by winning the battle of Avarayr, that when I was given a picture of him to colour in class, I shaded him all in black just to annoy my teacher. Later we read about early kings and their conquests, and recited verses by great Armenian poets like Hovhannes Tumanyan. We attended the Armenian church, but my mind would wander to the girls I fancied in the congregation and I never understood the service since it was conducted in an ancient version of the language that even some priests didn't understand.

In my teenage years my main concerns were kicking a football and watching films. Armenia was some faraway place and although I spoke proudly of it, I couldn't really claim to know it. I tried to justify my heritage to outsiders by pointing out famous Armenians in popular culture. 'Andre Agassi is Armenian,' I'd say. We weren't as proud of Cher. Of Youri Djorkaeff and Alain Boghossian: 'France wouldn't have won the 1998 World Cup without some Armenians in their squad.'

My family relocated to England when I was sixteen. The young Armenian community there would throw loud parties in a nightclub once a month, which I soon came to detest, so I distanced myself from them. I began to travel and found echoes of my background around the world. There is a bonding wherever two Armenians meet; an understanding that doesn't need to be spoken. At the Armenian Monastery of St Lazarus on an island near Venice, the priest immediately singled me out of the tour group and said, 'I know you're Armenian, I can tell from your eyes.' In India I stopped at an Armenian school in Calcutta, where early traders had set up communities along the Silk Road, and I played rugby with the students. In Buenos Aires I walked along Armenia Street, made new friends and went to watch River Plate play even though I was a secret Boca Juniors fan. On my previous visits to Armenia I had felt plenty of love but I had also felt like a stranger. I simply hadn't known enough, about who I was and where I had come from. But on this journey I felt that changing.

* * *

It had been a tough battle to get to the top of the pass, but what lay ahead of me was an endless downhill snaking down the mountain. This was going to be a lot of fun. I remounted the bike, gave it only the one pedal required, and sped off like the devil. From the start, I was flying down one bend and then another at breakneck speeds. My map said the ancient Selim *caravanserai* was nearby, a rare... blah... blah... blah...

I was having way too much fun to stop. I saw a small stone shack and wondered, what the hell is a *caravanserai* anyway? Just as I passed it, a large bee smacked me straight in the chest. At the speed I was going, it felt like someone had thrown a rock at me. At least I didn't swallow it, I thought, and kept going with a stupid, childish grin on my face.

I felt complete weightlessness, an indescribable freedom. With hardly any cars around, I was able to use the full extent of the road and expertly rounded the corkscrew turns at high speeds, then hunched over the handlebars to fly through the straights. Bend after bend appeared on this great descent until I reached a small village at the bottom of the valley with all the hair on my body standing up.

I stopped at a small shop and the owner said I was the first Armenian tourist he'd ever had come in. We spoke for a while, and he asked why anyone would cycle around the country. I told him to get a bike one day and ride it down the pass I'd just come through – then he'd understand. There was a young child in the shop eating ice cream. He stared at me with wide eyes the whole time I was there without blinking once.

I rode on down through the valley, stopping only when I was pulled over by a driver and his family who immediately opened the boot of their car and started handing me bags of fruit. At the next turn-off I suddenly noticed the heat. I had left the coolness of the mountain air behind me and was now in southern Armenia.

Finally I arrived at a great big sign announcing that I had reached the town of Yeghegnadzor. I checked into the hotel right alongside the sign and was immediately made to feel at home by the manager

Vahan and his father. The *kaghakabed* (city mayor) of Ashtarak – a town 150 kilometres away to the northwest – turned up. He was well dressed and had several gold chains and a Mercedes parked out front. He liked the idea of my trip and began chatting away to Vahan's father. I felt like a bystander in the conversation that followed:

'Are you married?'

'Of course he's not married! He's riding a bicycle around Armenia.'

The two of them carried on their discussion without me getting a word in, even though I was the topic.

The hotel was surrounded by fruit trees and had views of the mountains on every side. Vahan and his father had built the place themselves; they also had a construction business to repair run-down schools. As I was tucking into the five-course meal Vahan had prepared for me – *khorovadz*, cheese, salads, local wine, coffee and fruit – he told me about his kids. With two girls and now one newborn baby boy, he could stop reproducing, he said with a smile, because he had a son at last. I was exhausted after my long day and went easy on the wine, even though it was a local speciality and had apparently been a favourite of former French president Jacques Chirac when he visited the area. Vahan refused to let me pay for anything no matter how much I insisted.

Chapter 18

The Baron Of Jermuk

The warm, generous, and interesting people I was meeting on my ride around Armenia were becoming the big highlight of my trip. But if I had to pick one among all those special people, it would probably be Baron Ashot, owner of the Anush Hotel in Jermuk. Charismatic, in his late fifties, with white hair, a great moustache and a big round potbelly, he exuded authority. From the moment we met, I automatically addressed him as 'Baron' – the honorific term for respected elders. His baritone voice gave him a commanding presence, but there was a kindness in his eyes that made him very endearing. He welcomed me to his hotel like I was his long lost son and I liked him immediately.

It had been a two-day ride from Yeghegnadzor to Jermuk, via an overnight stop in the small city of Vayk, where I did some laundry, refuelled and found an Internet cafe to let my parents know I was still alive. A kid filled my tyres with air and they began to roll in perfect circles again. Soon after, I passed a couple of cycling tourists from Sao Paulo, Brazil; they were heading north and had just come up through Iran. The girl must have been a big hit there, I thought, with her short blonde hair and glacier-blue eyes.

The road to Jermuk climbed sharply from the start and wound up the cliffside in a ridiculously sheer gradient. A large green valley opened up, with golden flowers as far as the eye could see. To my left was a dramatic drop down to a large gorge with menacingly jagged edges. The road continued to rise. It was difficult to enjoy the scenery and keep my legs pumping. The heat grew intense and still the uphill continued. I was hurting, my legs felt like jelly, and all I wanted to do was rest.

Two hours later, I finally made it. I had always wanted to visit Jermuk, a spa town that's known for its clean air and the healing properties of its natural hot springs. The city's bottled water – also called 'Jermuk' – is distributed all over Armenia. The town enjoys a magnificent setting, positioned against a mountainous backdrop of lush green with dense forests in every direction. All in, it would make the perfect place for a day or two of relaxation.

High season was still weeks away and the town was quiet save for groups of fat Russian women waddling from sanitarium to sanitarium in search of super water. I made my way to the impressive colonnades in the town centre where you could sample the water for free. People visit from all over the world for this. A series of five metre-high stone vases lined the pillared passageway, fed by spouts bearing the life-giving waters. The vases were graded according to temperature, each one hotter than the last. Soft-spoken Artin, who had become my unofficial tour guide after bumping into me on the road, explained the whole process to me and told me to have a drink. I ignored the vendor trying to sell me an ornamental glass and bent over for a sip. Artin started me on the 35-degrees spout, which I thought was probably the girlie touristic one; I then worked my way up to the 55-degrees water, the one for real men. To be honest, it tasted like sulphuric piss water with a hint of rotten eggs. And it tasted worse and worse the hotter it got.

Next, Artin bought me what he called 'mountain gum', made by boiling the sap from the trees high up in the mountains. It was like I was chewing a tree. I believed him on the healthiness front though: anything that tasted this bad had to be good for you.

Ironically, in a town so full of flowing water, I was very dehydrated after my ride from Vayk. Artin offered to help find me a hotel, and that's how I ended up staying at the Anush with Baron Ashot and his wife, Digin Ashghen ('Digin' being the respectful term of address for an older woman). They were excited to have me as a guest and quoted me a ridiculously low price for a room. I had a whole floor to myself, with three different bedrooms (I didn't use any of them and slept on the couch) and a large living space.

I whiled away the afternoon drinking coffee and exchanging jokes with Baron Ashot in the hotel lobby. The more time I spent with him, the more he seemed to me to look like a larger retired version of Andranik, the revolutionary hero whose statue you see all over Armenia. During the repressive period of Ottoman rule in the late 1800s, Andranik became a symbol of Armenian resistance, organizing attacks against the Turks. Ever since, he has been idealized in poems, songs and stone – even by the Russians, who tried to erect a statue of him in the resort town of Sochi in 2011. The statue stayed up for one day before Turkey threatened to boycott the 2014 Sochi Winter Olympics unless it was taken down. Though I didn't share my thoughts about his twin with Baron Ashot, he would probably have enjoyed the comparison.

'I wish I was younger, I would have joined you on your trip,' he said, smiling. And then, looking serious, 'Are you married?' He suggested I should marry one of the two lovely girls from Alaverdi that were currently staying at the hotel. One of them was a businesswoman, apparently, who suffered from migraines and was hoping the Jermuk waters would help.

'Why not?' I said abruptly, which made him laugh.

Baron Ashot didn't get married until he was thirty-five, and he gave me the same advice his father had offered him: '*Ov vor ulla arr, arten pooshman es.*' In other words, just take anyone: you're already doomed, no matter what. He laughed heartily at this, and then looked around to make sure his wife wasn't anywhere nearby. He twisted his whiskers and said family was important, that a tree that bears no fruit gets pulled out by the roots and discarded.

He liked to talk about business. He told me of a man who emigrated from Karabagh to Malaysia in the 1800s and became so wealthy there that he tried to buy Karabagh from the Russians. He couldn't figure out how, in that day and age, someone could amass so much wealth in Malaysia. We went through some theories, but none of them seemed to satisfy him.

My legs were tired and it was suggested that I book an appointment with the hotel masseuse, a middle-aged woman named Gohar. She had the air of a retired witch doctor. With her frizzy blonde shoulder-length hair and roundish figure, she would have looked perfect behind a crystal ball or a pack of Tarot cards. I'd had some massages in Asia, where tiny but tough women had beaten me to within an inch of my life. But I never felt any different after and was always left feeling rather uneasy about the whole process. I'm a fairly relaxed person and tend to see massages as being for people that are stressed all the time. What used to annoy me the most in China and Thailand was that they always played soft meditative music as they pummelled and walked all over you, when heavy metal would have been much more fitting. Still, my knees were in pain and I thought that was a good reason to give it another try.

Gohar took out a bottle of olive oil and drenched me with it until I felt like a mixed-leaf salad in an Italian restaurant. She worked on my muscles then took out a wooden roller to flatten me out like fresh pasta. She did a few arm twists and turns and laughed when I cried out in pain. 'And you call yourself an athlete!' she hollered. I'm pretty sure she kept my bum out in the open much longer than she had to, but I didn't mind making an old lady happy.

In a further attempt to ease my aching body, I looked for a place to have a swim. At the reception desk of the swanky Hotel Armenia I was greeted by a woman so beautiful it made me flatulent. I paid next to nothing to swim around all afternoon and use the sauna in surroundings designed to resemble a Roman bathhouse. One of the staff also showed me the gym, which had an exercise bike as the centrepiece. I explained that a bike was the last thing I wanted to see at the moment.

In the evening, I took a stroll to the artificial lake in the town centre and stopped at a small circular cafe for a beer. To my surprise the cafe was also a boat. Soon, without any warning, we set sail, making rapid little circles in the moonlight. Seasickness tablets wouldn't have helped, but if you'd graduated the Teacups ride at Disneyland you would have felt right at home. Round and round we spun, which made having a quiet beer very problematic. We danced this dance for what

131

seemed like ages and I felt like a hostage forced to order more drinks until we reached dry land. What a circus.

It was getting late and I hadn't eaten much all day. I queued up at a shop around the corner where a man was busily chopping hunks of meat and chunks of cheese for what appeared to be a pretty indecisive crowd. There were five other shops on the same street, but I liked this man's energy and waited my turn while the customers in front of me tasted every one of his village cheeses. Eventually Girayr got to me and my order, which took all of thirty seconds. He was really happy to have me in his shop, he said, and immediately broke out a bottle of fine vodka and chopped up some pickled cucumbers his father had prepared. We began to toast everything and everyone. A customer came in and Girayr briskly told him to come back later.

He told me about his life as a schoolteacher and how little it paid. How he was forced to have a shop to provide for his family. He pulled out his Armenian history textbooks and began to give me a lesson. He said most of our richest heritage had been lost to Turkey, that they had destroyed the remains of our old kingdoms and erased our history. He tried his best to tell his students about our past, he said, and wished he could just concentrate on teaching. As we drank and ate the delicious cucumbers, we shared more stories. He was such a bundle of energy and a wonderful host. As I was about to return to my hotel, he packed a few extra cucumbers in my bag and we drank a final shot of vodka to toast our good health.

* * *

132

I attempted to drink the spring waters again the next day… Blekhh! The sun was shining bright, so I took a long walk around Jermuk and watched the reflection of the trees dancing on the lake. Strolling down a beautifully scenic wooded path with the sound of flowing water all around, I felt glad to be there. I passed a small park full of statues of well-known Armenian figures and gave a nod to Andranik, smiling again at his uncanny resemblance to Baron Ashot. The whiskers were just as wise, the eyes just as determined, and they both had the sort of noble face that can inspire you to greater things.

Further up the road I got a good view of the bridge that had brought me into Jermuk the day before. It stood at a magnificent height above the gorge. Each time a car crossed, it would rumble violently, making me hold the railings nervously. Down the jagged cliff face far below I could just make out the Jermuk Waterfall that everyone went on about. It didn't look like anything to get excited about and I decided it wasn't worth the long climb down. Instead I went for a relaxing coffee outside the Hotel Armenia. Men sat discussing business as mothers wiped ice cream off their children. Everyone seemed to be carrying a jug of that vile water to constantly refuel throughout the day.

I spent the afternoon sitting with Baron Ashot again. He was still mulling over the businessman from Karabagh who made it rich in Malaysia. 'What is there in Malaysia?' he muttered to the wind. An eccentric thin-framed woman with ragged dark hair entered the lobby and asked Baron Ashot how he was getting on with a book she had lent him. He looked very confused as she started speaking about the healing power of pyramids. As soon as she left, Baron Ashot made a face and said he couldn't get his head around the book. 'It says you have to have sex with God in order to find healing,' he said, sighing awkwardly. Then, opening his eyes as wide as they would go, he blurted out, 'Who would write such a thing!'

Gohar the masseuse turned up and we began discussing the origins of mankind. Baron Ashot argued that Noah's Ark had landed on Mount Ararat, making everyone in the world originally Armenian. I countered with my own theory that judging by the general hairiness of the Armenian male, we were living proof that we came from the apes. Gohar laughed ferociously at that – I'm guessing because she had seen many an Armenian man naked on her massage table – and agreed. Darwin can't have ever met an Armenian, I told them. If he had, he never would have bothered to sail to the Galapagos. In fact, on the Darwin chart of evolution, we're hunched over somewhere around the middle when it comes to hairiness and politics.

For dinner I ordered *khinkali* from the hotel restaurant – soft yellow Georgian dumplings stuffed with beef that's heavily spiced with herbs, onions and garlic. The meat is raw when its bundled inside the dough to be steamed, causing the juices to be trapped inside. The top of each dumpling comes with a stem, as this is food to be eaten by hand. You pick it up and quickly suck in all the juices at first bite, otherwise you risk turning your tablecloth into a Jackson Pollock painting.

To round off the evening I paid a final visit to Girayr's shop. He pulled out the vodka as soon as he saw me, got rid of his customers and this time sliced up a length of heavily cured *basturma*. Oh, God, I thought. Another smelly three days.

Chapter 19

You'll Always Have A Friend In Jermuk

'I'm not sure if they want Armenian champagne that costs $5 or French that costs $200,' Baron Ashot said after he put the phone down. Someone had called to book a room for a honeymooning couple, asking for champagne and flowers. He expected to see me in Jermuk again when I got married, he said. I told him to have the champagne and roses ready. As I readied my bike, he gathered the staff together and they saw me off by throwing a bucket of water down the steps outside. It's an old Armenian tradition to wish someone a safe journey, the idea being that everything will flow smoothly, just like the water. I wouldn't have got better treatment at any of the finest hotels in the world.

I was feeling good being back on the bike with my newly limber knees. As I exited the town, three road sweepers having breakfast looked up at me in surprise. The old man yelled at me to stop, and excitedly asked if he could ride the bike. He hopped on and started to go down the road as the two ladies laughed their heads off. They thought my trip was crazy but also wonderful, and invited me to join them for breakfast. I thanked them, but had to move on. If I had accepted every invitation to eat or drink so far I'd still be in Yerevan.

I got through the first few uphills knowing I had a long downward stretch to look forward to after the final one. Just as I reached the very last climb, with my legs pumping hard, out of nowhere a kid pulled out from behind me on his bike and started to pedal past me. His name was Manoug. He said he was fifteen but I was pretty sure he was no more than twelve. His voice was soft and his black hair nearly reached his eyebrows. He asked if I wanted to stop for *sourj* (coffee) and I couldn't say no to another bike enthusiast. I asked if he wanted to switch bikes on the ride back and he accepted with a big grin on his face.

His small bike was in tatters. Its black paint was chipped all over, the wheels had lost alignment many moons ago and the pedals swung around wildly. He had made some admirable modifications, adding CDs to the wheels to act as reflectors and doing some handcrafted wiring to make a cage at the back to carry things in. We rode back down the hill to a dirt path that led to a private piece of land with a caravan trailer parked and a concrete barn next to it. Manoug ran inside to make coffee and I sat outside staring down at the rich valley of grazing cows and the gorge on the horizon. He asked if I liked milk and motioned me to come inside the barn. Grabbing a bucket, he expertly caught one of the scurrying goats and began to milk it. He offered me a go. I was confident I'd seen enough movies to bluff my way through, so I pulled, lost all direction and the milk went all over Manoug's trousers. The goat got restless, realizing it was dealing with an amateur, and after a few more tries and another tick against the bucket list, I let the professional take over. Heated and with a spoonful of sugar, the milk tasted delicious.

Manoug was so enthusiastic about cycling and I could see he was thinking of ways to keep me around longer. I decided I would try and buy him a new bike if possible, and asked if there was a shop around. I needed some parts, I told him. Manoug said sure, but we should go riding in the cow tunnel first. I had no idea what he was on about, but how can you say no when someone gives you an invitation like that.

The tunnel was near the barn, a small concrete bunker with a trickle of a stream flowing through it that apparently came all the way from Goris, about 100 kilometres away. Cows huddled inside it, out of the sun, and stared at us impassively as we rode around in circles. I tried hard to hold onto the walls when I stopped, to keep my feet dry, but that didn't always work. It was a unique scenario, and a really enjoyable one, and I would highly recommend it under 'things to do' the next time I'm on TripAdvisor.

Manoug asked me to come to his home, back down the hill towards Jermuk. On the way his single handbrake broke. He said not to worry, that he would just use his feet to slow down instead. Including Manoug, there were six kids in the family. His mother looked tired, and I didn't blame her. We sat down together for coffee while she brought out apricots, fresh yogurt, cheese, tomatoes and ice cream. I saw that they had a fancy cable TV box and found the Tour de France on it. Manoug had never heard of it, and the sight of cyclists climbing the high mountains with their superbikes amazed him. His father shyly invited me to come and see his new grass mower. It used to take him months to cut enough grass to feed his cows through the winter, but with the new machine it would only take two weeks.

Manoug and I took a walk into the village and to the little patch of garden where the family grew vegetables. He began to pick strawberries and small carrots for us to eat. We walked to the lake where a small, ancient church stood at the water's edge. I got out my camera to snap some pictures, and then asked Manoug if he would like to take some. He liked the idea instantly and started clicking away at me, then the church, then the cows, and finally the flowers. After each picture he'd give me the camera and wait for a critique. He actually had a pretty good eye and I didn't have to lie when I said his shots were good.

Later we rode to the bike shop, which turned out to be a shop like any other in Armenia, selling mainly alcohol, bread and candy. They had a few bikes for small children, and Manoug said they had some bike parts in the back I could look at. I found some new brakes for his bike and two new tyres and asked if there was anything else that he'd like. He was surprised and asked what I was doing. I replied that he was a good kid and had fed me and shown me around all day, and I wanted to do something small for him. He felt shy about accepting my gifts, but inside he was excited about all the new additions. He very timidly asked if he could get a spray can of gold paint to colour his bike, and I said done. I was just disappointed I couldn't get him a new bike entirely.

Down the road from the shop some kids were playing football and I went to join them. Manoug said he would rather ride my bike for a bit, if that was all right, and I said sure. I joined the game on the dirt field as we picked teams and played against a single goalkeeper. The ball had become unstitched and the rubber was sticking out at one end like a tumour. It was impossible to direct it when you kicked it and I embarrassed myself badly a few times, even falling on my backside once after slipping on the dirt. Still, I scored a few and it was good to kick a ball around again. The kids didn't ask where I was from or why I wasn't married. We just played the game. It was nice to be accepted without any questions.

Manoug returned from his ride and we rode back to the caravan with his new tyres on his handlebars and his brakes and paint in a bag swinging in the wind. He couldn't wait to attach everything. He made more coffee and said I should stay there that night and leave in the morning. But I needed to get on the road to Sisian to get through the high pass the next day. I gave him my number and wished him the best of luck. His eyes filled a little, and as I rode off he yelled out, 'Remember, you'll always have a friend here in Jermuk.'

* * *

The downhill began. With a sharp tailwind behind me, I raced along at incredible speeds. I didn't even have to pedal on the up slopes. The sun was glimmering through the soft clouds, making the fields and flowers glow as far as the eye could see. I swooped and swerved between the great mountains as the wind filled my ears with a deafening noise. I knew that I'd miss this place.

In no time at all I had covered the twenty-odd kilometres back onto the main road to Sisian. At the Darp Hotel I was greeted by twin-brother chefs and an old caretaker, Arsen, who laughed after everything he said. It was a beautiful riverside spot with the sounds of running water everywhere and a scattering of secluded picnic tables. We sat down by a tree and

Arsen ordered us a beer. He asked about life in England and let out loud ooohs and ahhhs at my every comment. When the waitress came with the beer, he said, 'Our boy here needs a wife, how's your daughter?'

'She's sixteen,' she replied discouragingly.

Arsen turned to me with a wry smile and said, 'Ooh, she's sixteen,' like that was a selling point, then laughed his head off. I felt like I had some catching up to do with the drinking.

The clouds began to rumble and within seconds it was raining heavily. Customers came hurrying inside out of the downpour and Arsen busied himself trying to help them out. He came back after a while, kicking open the door, soaked from head to toe. With the rain pelting down behind him, he yelled out at the top of his voice, 'This is all your fault! You brought your English weather with you!' And he laughed like a crazy man.

The twin brothers used an ingenious subterranean barbecue pit to cook their meat. They lowered long skewers of meat into the stone pit, and then secured a steel lid over the hole to lock in all the flavours. Seeing how busy they were, I said I could sit anywhere and that they shouldn't treat me like a guest. I was led to the back kitchen where all the bread and vegetables were prepared and was brought a beautiful plate of *khorovadz*. The staff kept coming in and checking on me between frantically filling orders.

Arsen led a couple and their extremely beautiful daughter through the kitchen and into another dining area. On his way back through, he turned to me wide-eyed and asked, 'You want that one?' loud enough that the parents could hear him in the other room. Then he giggled. I just smiled an embarrassed stupid grin, but I surely *did* want that one.

Back in my room, my phone rang and it was Manoug calling to ask if he could come to Sisian with me the next day. It was hard to tell him no, but I promised he would have plenty adventures of his own one day.

Chapter 20

Inheritance Of Stick Figures

The road to Sisian was carved through a deep gorge and left little to no room for cyclists. For fifty-five kilometres I fought cars and lorries for every millimetre of space. The traffic was continuous, mainly large trucks, as this was the main route for goods being transported between Armenia and Iran. To make it worse, it was badly paved with a cheap tarmac blend that was hard on my tyres.

The climb got steeper and steeper as I wound my way up to the Vorotan Pass separating the Vayots Dzor region from Syunik. Every time I turned a corner and glanced up at the next horizon, another set of hills greeted me, breaking my heart a little. Another set of jagged peaks and small villages scattered across the mountainside. It was relentless. A driver pulled up and asked if I wanted a lift to the top, but I hadn't come all this way to be driven around, no matter how enticing the invitation at that moment.

The large eighteen-wheelers ruled that road. The truck drivers were slow and careful; it was the people trying to overtake them that were the real danger. They would see me in the opposite lane but would still recklessly decide it was a good time to pass the massive lorry, missing me only by a whisker. I would just shake my head in disapproval, expressing myself with sophisticated English reserve. Then I'd see another string of gravestones by the side of the road and wonder if they'd be next. Or me.

Two high towers marked the gateway to Syunik and

finally my exhausting four-hour ordeal was over. I had made it to the top of the 2,300-metre pass. Staring down deep into the heart of the valley, I saw the point I had started from.

I thought it would be a nice easy downhill from there, but I was wrong. The road was filled with a bone-shaking rattle of cracks, bumps and extremely large potholes. I had to concentrate hard to navigate past all the obstacles. My eyes were scanning every centimetre of road ahead as I swerved around hazards and anticipated every bump. I was only dimly aware of the beautiful green valley as I rolled through it, eyes on the road, with glimpses of blue in the distance from a large reservoir. A worker I passed called out to tell me to be careful. A cyclist up there had been hit by a car last year and there were a lot of drunk drivers about, he said. They can't be any worse than when they're sober, I replied.

I finally shook, rattled and rolled into town. Children swimming in the river near the road whistled and shouted at me to join them. I was too tired to consider it and kept riding until I reached the lovely tree-lined streets of Sisian. There was a peacefulness about the place and I liked it as soon as I arrived. Water fountains and a variety of monuments heralded the well-preserved main square, and just beyond was the Hotel Dina. As this had floral gardens and apple trees – two of my mother's favourite things – I decided it was a good choice for the night.

That evening I chose a quiet, empty restaurant for dinner. The waiter, excited at the sight of a customer, turned on the music, and it was soon raining Russian pop once again, a noise that should only ever be heard in back-alley eastern European discos and torture chambers. It seemed I had started a trend, as a solitary older gentleman turned up soon after me and sat down. It was unusual to see someone else dining alone. His name was Roupen and he was originally of Armenian descent although he lived in Paris. He said he had come to Armenia to feel young again. He was very well travelled and we shared stories from the road and found we had plenty in common. A lot about him seemed lonely and I wondered if that was how I would end up when I was in my fifties.

Roupen found Armenia changed this time, he said, and much less optimistic. 'The people used to be happier,' he told me, but now there was discontent and many Armenians wanted to run off to Russia. This tallied with what I'd found too. I'd been told that though the official population of Armenia was put at three million, in actual fact it was barely two and a half, when you took account of all the emigrants. Things had long been difficult in Armenia, but it seemed they might now be at breaking point.

* * *

Chubby, kind-hearted Dikran was to be my driver for the day. We drove out of Sisian in his Soviet 4x4 and up to his village of Ishkhanasar on a rocky, bumpy road. He was happy I spoke Armenian – the last person he'd driven was Spanish and they'd sat in silence for hours. 'You are a good Armenian,' he observed, commenting on how well I spoke the language. 'It's good you want to come and see your country.' I told him not to treat the day like work, more like two friends travelling together. Within minutes, the fact I wasn't married came up. He was

144

shocked. 'You should marry my daughter, she's an interpreter,' he said rather casually. Jesus, I thought, I must make quite an impression in the first five minutes I meet people.

The route up into the Syunik mountains took us into a heavenly world full to the brim with wild flowers of every colour. The road climbed to 3,300 metres and some of the higher sections were still snowbound; it's only open a few months of the year and we were one of the first cars to get through that season.

We reached Ughtasar, nestled in between the cliff faces. On two sides were snow-covered mountaintops; in the middle was a lake surrounded by lush fields. The whites, greens and blues were the picture of perfection. It was stunning. I couldn't help but be reminded of Patagonia, and had never imagined such a place existed in Armenia.

We walked along the rocks near the iceberg-blue lake and Dikran pointed out the ancient carvings etched into some of the flat pieces of black volcanic stone scattered in front of us. The drawings were simple, only a few millimetres deep, and broke my personal rule about what is and what is not art. I came up with my rule when wandering through the Tate Modern museum in London. It is simple: if I can draw it, it's not art. I'm a master of stick figures and nothing else. (I can also paint a canvas in a single colour.) Still, I was forgiving about these petroglyphs due to the fact that they were from 12,000 BC. Perhaps they were the work of my own ancestors, who had passed me their gift for stick figures.

A stick man with a bow stood in front of some four-legged stick animals with tails. Their size seemed highly exaggerated. It was hard to imagine people living here so long ago, wanting to leave a small legacy behind with their drawings. 'That's a bull,' Dikran said. 'That's a celebration. That's a man hunting.' He wasn't a historian and I was glad because a history lesson might have ruined the place.

Back in the car, Dikran swatted away about a hundred giant flies that had come in through the open window. We returned down the mountain, stopping every time Dikran spotted a mushroom, so he could jump out and pick it. At every halt we'd collect a fresh set of fifty flies, which would get shooed out just in time for the next mushroom stop.

We reached the bottom with a giant bag of fungi and were off to Karahunj, known as the Armenian Stonehenge, though it's hardly the organized circle of rocks like the one in England. Standing at two and a half metres tall, there are over fifty stones scattered across the area. Each is broader at the bottom than the top, and narrows to a point like a pear. They date back to the Bronze Age and may have some connection with astronomy, though nobody has yet been able to link it to any recognizable sun patterns of constellations.

One of the highlights of the day was making a new friend in Dikran. We discussed every subject under the Armenian sun – what it meant to be Armenian, the importance of marrying an Armenian and raising your family to be good Armenians – and he was adamant that he wouldn't live anywhere other than Sisian. But it was tough trying to make ends meet. He worked hard – as a driver, a shop owner, a construction worker and a farmer.

Back at the hotel he gave me the bag of

mushrooms and said the hotel would cook them for me. I went inside and handed over the bag. I didn't want to break Dikran's heart and tell him I didn't like mushrooms so I instructed the staff to tell him that I had enjoyed them immensely, were he ever to ask.

In the evening I met Dikran at one of the outdoor cafes under the trees near my hotel and we ordered a round of beers. We felt like brothers now. We tucked into some *lahmajunes*, thin circles of flattened dough topped with spicy minced lamb that are sometimes described as Armenian pizza, sometimes Turkish pizza, depending on whom you're talking to. Dikran asked if I would come back to town for his birthday in September. To sweeten the deal, he said he'd have a nice potential wife waiting for me if I did.

Chapter 21

Before You're Thirty!

It had been a restless night, thanks to Celine Dion. The cafe next door to my hotel had belted out her five 'best' tracks over and over into the small hours. I'm usually exceedingly patient, but something about 'My Heart Will Go On' irritates the hell out of me. So I wasn't in the best of moods to tackle the reckless drivers, bad asphalt and relentless headwind out of Sisian. The first twenty kilometres were a real struggle. I was fumbling on my easiest gears with the wind pushing me back and I could barely manage any speed at all. But just as Dikran had said, the next twenty kilometres sloped all the way down to Goris. As a plus, the wind shifted and I was soon soaring, more than making up for my slow start.

The landscape went from nondescript dry earth, to a small patch of green fields, then back to barren wasteland. Dark clouds gathered over the mountains on my left and were brewing an ugly black. I gripped my handlebars tightly and swerved through the terrain, avoiding as many thumps and potholes as I could. It became a quick and easy ride with the earlier irritations long forgotten. Very soon I was staring down at the orange cliffs that encircled Goris.

The streets of the city centre were teeming with children carrying large buckets. I realized I had arrived on Vartavar, the day of the annual water festival. The festival has pagan origins associated with Astghik, the goddess of water, beauty, love and fertility. Centuries ago, Armenians would offer up roses as part of their religious devotions to Astghik (*vart* in Vartavar means 'rose'). In the Christian tradition, it became customary to throw buckets of water instead (much safer than roses). It was as though every child in the city knew I was coming: one by one, full buckets greeted me as I pedalled through town. Everyone cheered as I got soaked head to toe in continual waves of water. Some of the kids were shy about splashing a stranger, but I could tell they really wanted to, so I ducked my head down invitingly to let them know it was okay.

I settled into the Mirhav Hotel, the most tastefully designed place I'd seen in Armenia. The owner was a retired Iranian-Armenian surgeon and with the decor had made good use of his steady hand and eye for detail. Over coffee in the garden he told me about a cycling trip from Iran to Armenia he had done with a friend when he was seventeen, which must have been about fifty years ago. He described the roads back then and laughingly said how lucky I was now. He told stories about the kindness he'd received in the villages he passed through, and I was glad that hadn't changed.

Next morning I was greeted with an extravagant breakfast of eggs, cows and sheep's cheese, thin *lavash* bread, apricot jam, apricot juice, apricots themselves, and good coffee. Taxi driver Smbad turned up in a beat-up car that had seen better days, ready to take me to the Monastery of Tatev. There was no need to wear a seatbelt in this car – Smbad said he had that all taken care of, with tinted windows so the police couldn't see inside. He went into a state of shock when he found out I wasn't married. For a moment I thought he might swerve off the road. 'You better get started soon,' he shouted. 'I'll only give you till you're thirty!' His kids and grandkids were his main source of happiness in life. He was expecting a new granddaughter that day and was waiting for the phone call.

He told me about the Monastery of Tatev, but with a flash of anger in his voice he said, 'I don't like all this religion business. Buddha, Jesus, Muhammad, and the one the Indians like with all the arms, they're all the same — it's just important to have faith in a creator. Otherwise life is meaningless.' Then he went into a long rant about ridiculous priests, and one in particular in his hometown that liked to wear skinny jeans on his days off. Smbad still liked the churches for their beauty and history, but cursed the people within their walls as charlatans.

We passed a large shoe factory to our right that Smbad said had once put a thousand people to work. Its doors were now shut forever. Pointing to his left, where the wheat was waving in the breeze, he said, 'Everyone would have left the area after the factory closed if the fields hadn't been good for farming.' Nonetheless, his son had emigrated and was living in Moscow. He was doing quite well working in construction and kept pleading with his father to go and join him. But Smbad simply couldn't. 'For better or worse, this is my home,' he said solemnly as he dropped me off at the Wings of Tatev.

This recently finished cable car was now the longest reversible aerial tramway in the world, climbing 320 metres above a gorge to the Tatev Monastery, hidden high up in the mountains. The cable car operators seemed to have been chosen after a very careful selection process, with the main requirement being that you had to be a very beautiful woman. I talked to Hermine, who operated the buttons, and tried feebly to break the ice by asking if she got tired of going back and forth the same way all day. She smiled and said no, she liked it. We passed over a river and Satan's Bridge, towering high above the landscape as the monastery crept closer in the distance. It was all very impressive, even though I hardly looked at the scenery. Hermine was a World Heritage site on her own.

Tatev Monastery itself was truly one of the most amazing places I'd ever seen. It's built in such an impossible location, perched on the edge of a cliff overlooking a deep gorge through which the Vorotan River rumbles far, far below. The magnificent ninth-century monastery is enclosed within fortified walls and comprises three churches, a library, a dining hall, a mausoleum and several other administrative buildings. Over the centuries it was raided by the usual suspects – Seljuk Turks, Mongols – and was badly damaged by a number of earthquakes. But at one time more than a thousand monks lived there, and from the 1300s to the 1400s it was a university and a place of learning. During my visit, a priest was singing in the main church, making the most of the acoustics, his voice resonating around the large stone space. Intricately carved crosses lined nearly every wall and the narrow passageways of beige brick led to ancient halls with wonderful views of the mountains.

Smbad drove me back to town and as he dropped me off at the Mirhav Hotel, shouted, 'Remember, before you're thirty! Then come back and pay us a visit'! Goris was now glowing in the sunshine and I found a pleasant outdoor cafe overlooking the mountains, with a good view of the ancient caves that peppered the slopes. They looked like the mounds of giant termites. During the Karabagh War Goris was heavily shelled and many people took refuge in these ancient hollows, watching as their homes were destroyed.

I made sure to get back to the hotel in time for the Tour de France highlights programme. I needed all the inspiration I could get before the next day's ride to Karabagh. This last leg of my journey was going to take all the mental and physical strength I had. I was heading for one of the more beautiful areas in the world, full of ancient Armenian monasteries and dramatic landscapes but with a recent history shadowed by war. I took what I didn't need out of my bags to make things as light as possible. I thought about the nearly 900 kilometres I'd covered in just under a month, all the people I had met along the way, and what lay ahead.

Chapter 22

Into Karabagh

I had set my alarm for 6 a.m. and by 6.15 I was off. As I pedalled the steep climb out of Goris, the mountains cast their dawn shadows over the city and I was suddenly filled with apprehension at the task ahead. I reached the top as the first rays of sun started to illuminate the light brown rooftops below. Turning my back on Goris, I began the forty-kilometre roll down the other side of the mountain. The tarmac was newly laid and Sayat Nova swam beautifully over it. Curving around the winding roads I felt a thrill like no other. The air was still, there were no cars, and the road just kept dropping and dropping. I gave my brakes the morning off and enjoyed the exhilarating speeds and picturesque surroundings.

A monument announced that I was now in Karabagh and I stared down a long range of mountains at its magnificence. The palette of colours was like nothing I had yet seen on this trip, every shade seeming richer and born from a more fertile earth in these valleys of dreams. I could see the sweep of my road cutting through the landscape, an apparently endless downhill ribbon of tarmac. Technically I wasn't in Armenia any more, I was now in the Nagorno-Karabagh Republic, a piece of land populated almost entirely by Armenians, a land Armenians know by its ancient name, Artsakh, whose kingdom was founded in 189 BC. I rested on a bench to take in the moment, gazing down at what the international community considers an unrecognized no man's land. This place of such serene beauty, that has seen so much fighting and bloodshed.

For six years, from 1988–94, the strip of land between Armenia and Azerbaijan was fought over by both countries in a gruesome conflict that came to be known as the Nagorno-Karabagh War. The region once belonged to the earliest Armenian kingdoms and there are still relics from that period, along with historic monasteries. After the First World War, the Russians went back and forth on the issue until Joseph Stalin decided to pass the land over to the Azeris in the 1920s as a political move to please Turkey. Azerbaijan is a Turkic state and has long been seen by Armenians as almost an extension of Turkey, to the point that Armenians call all Azeris Turks. The region remained under Soviet control, however, and because of that it stayed peaceful. But in 1988, when the Soviet Union began to weaken and borders began to be drawn for countries about to gain their independence, this strip of land became a major issue. Disagreements heated up very quickly and it turned into a battle zone. Horrific acts of violence were committed by both sides. The Armenian army was half the size of the Azeri military, and had a much smaller arsenal, but they succeeded in winning back the region. 'Because it wasn't their land they were fighting for,' an Armenian former soldier once told me when explaining how they had overcome the odds.

I said goodbye to the angry one-eyed dog that had joined me on my bench, hopped on the bike, and didn't pedal a single revolution for the next forty-five minutes. I simply screamed and sang down the road. A sign said that Mr Karapetyan had paid for this road to be newly paved, and I thanked him. There was nothing but lush green fields all around and the road was mine. I used both lanes for the big winding turns and imagined I was in the Tour de France, breaking away from the peloton, trying to take the yellow jersey. The thirty-five kilometres to the border crossing flew by in no time at all.

I was slightly worried about how the border officials would react to a cyclist and wondered if they might even not let me through. But I was greeted by an uninterested guard who simply motioned for me to pull over, looked at my passport, scribbled something in his book, which was hand-written like he was making notes in his personal diary, then waved me on. I stopped at the cafe next to his office and was pretty happy with myself for having covered so much ground. There's nothing like a good downhill to make you optimistic about life.

That optimism was short lived. As soon as I reached the city of Berdzor, the road shot up steeply for as far as I could see. But it was still only 11 a.m. and I felt strong for having reached the halfway point to Stepanakert, the capital of Karabagh. Towards the top of Berdzor I met some kids, one of whom looked admiringly at the bike. He said he loved cycling so I let him have a go, and he whizzed up the incline with no effort at all. He was amazed how easy it was to ride and I blushed a little at how much better he rode it than me.

I spent the next four hours walking my bike up steep mountain roads. As strong as my legs had got over the last month, the weight I was carrying and the severe gradients were just too much. The sun beat down and the heat was unbearable. I tried thinking about how wonderful it would feel to reach

Stepanakert. I imagined Sayat Nova and me standing proudly before the Dadik Babik statue, a symbol of the city and the end of our journey. My goal had always been to make it to Karabagh, and now it seemed so close and yet so very far. A part of me felt like a failure. I should have been able to *ride* this road. I tried a few times, but the gradient was just too extreme and I felt like I needed more gears – twenty-one more to be exact. So I walked on.

As I turned along a cliff, far off in the distance I saw the edge of a mountain that seemed like the final high point of the climb. A farmer came past me on his horse and confirmed that that was indeed the last of it, and that it was straight down to Stepanakert from there. It was a torturous final ascent. Everything began to hurt and the complacency of being so near the end set in as I came closer to the ridge. I reached the summit exhausted and sweating heavily. I stopped at a cafe for some ice cream and drinks to restore all the lost calories. A crowd gathered round to ask about the bike and find out if I was crazy. One man said he'd seen me on the road and asked why I had been walking and not riding. I told him the bike was there if he wanted to give it a go himself and the crowd laughed. I wasn't in the mood for conversation. I was exhausted and wanted to continue to the finish line. Everyone confirmed what the farmer had told me: it was all downhill from there on.

So I climbed back on and rode hard, sprinting the first hundred metres, then flying down the mountain. The breeze from all the speed lifted my spirits and I was loving life again. My brakes were by now exhausted to near nothingness so I had to anticipate my braking points early as I swished through the sharp turns and ate up the kilometres. A lot of people had told me it would be too difficult to ride to Karabagh, that the roads would be too tough, but here I was. I knew I was going to make it, and it felt good.

The road to Stepanakert rolled straight down as far as I could see. Catching a glimpse of the city nestled in the valley below made me smile. I turned the last few sharp corners carelessly overtaking cars, and then I was there. I took a back road that bypassed the centre and led straight to the Dadik Babik statue on the other side of town. Its two proud, massive faces, a grandmother and grandfather with heads shaped like mountains, stood in front of me. Sayat and I had arrived in triumph. It was equivalent to arriving in Paris on the final day of the Tour De France and standing proudly on the finish line on the Champs-Elysees having completed the tour.

I thought of all the roads I'd conquered to get there. All the great people I had met along the way. I knew this would be where I'd say goodbye to Sayat Nova. He had been a worthy companion and had held up miraculously well over the last 1,000 kilometres, without a single puncture. I thanked the guy that had recommended me the tyres at Evans cycling shop back home in Chiswick. Sure, Sayat's brakes had lost their grip and he was covered in dust and dung, but he had a fighting spirit. I couldn't have asked for more.

Chapter 23

Skinny Legs

Kristinae, the sweet and lovely receptionist at the Dghyak Hotel in Stepanakert, made very good coffee – often a make or break factor in a traditional Armenian marriage. We'd had a nice chat the evening before, though I'd had to cut it short sooner than I would have liked because I was so exhausted. Today I was full of energy. I asked if she had any brothers, but quickly realized that in Armenia this question usually precedes a marriage proposal, or is at least an attempt to gauge how many people are likely to discipline you if you step out of line. Before her brain had time to start running a montage of what our lives together might be like, I quickly explained I was hoping she had a younger brother that might want a bicycle. She laughed and said she only had three sisters.

I told her I was finished riding and Sayat Nova was hers if she wanted him. Her grin broadened and turned into a large smile. She had always wanted to learn how to ride a bicycle, she said. Then she turned a bit shy and said people didn't simply gift such things there. I had no intention of selling it to one of the privileged few who could afford it, and I wasn't going to take advantage of anyone who *couldn't* afford it. I told Kristinae to use it well. Whether she wanted to ride him or sell him, just let Sayat Nova bring her happiness.

I headed off to apply for my Karabagh visa. It's a bit unusual, but the system is to do this *after* you arrive, not at the border. Some people had told me not to bother, that the whole thing was a joke, run by crooks. Sure enough, it was a shambles inside the office, full of tour groups trying to find a pen and fill out the forms. I completed mine, handed it in and waited… and waited… Eventually a young lady came out of the office and said my visa was ready. I waved my arms in the air victoriously, but the Russian tour group didn't find it funny. It was a tough crowd, and that's why nobody's ever heard of a Russian stand-up comedian.

As I strolled around central Stepanakert in the pleasant summer warmth, a grey-haired man in a plaid shirt shyly stopped me to ask about my camera. His name was Garik and he took passport photos for a living. At his shop, located just off the main road, he showed me his own camera, a taped-up fading SLR that had worked hard in its time. He worried about something happening to it since he couldn't afford another one. He asked if I wanted a beer. My watch said 11 a.m., but my throat said why not. Garik hurried across the road and brought back two cans. 'I know you don't need a glass, because you drink it straight from the can in England,' he said with confidence.

A thin old man entered the shop looking slightly frazzled. Garik introduced him as his brother and asked if he wanted to have a beer with us. He refused in a way that suggested he never touched the stuff. Then he pulled half a litre of vodka out of his trouser pocket and poured himself a glass. When Garik explained that I was from England, the brother looked at me with great seriousness and asked, 'Can you bring me something back from England?' I asked what he had in mind. 'A woman!' he said in a loud yearning voice and Garik and I laughed. By now Haik, a young guy who ran the car parts shop next door had joined us and was enjoying the conversation. 'What sort of woman would you like?' I asked out of curiosity. 'Tall, short, blonde, brunette?' He interrupted my questioning abruptly. 'Skinny legs!' He said he didn't care about anything else as long as her legs were skinny.

When I brought up the subject of the bike, Garik's face lit up. In his youth he had been something of a cycling specialist, he said. Back in 1973, when the Armenian football team Ararat had played in the Soviet Union cup final – still the greatest achievement in Armenian football to date – he had vowed to stand on his bike and keep his balance for the full ninety minutes. He achieved it, but was drafted into the army the next day and hasn't ridden a bike since. 'Bring your bike tomorrow,' he said, 'and I'll ride again and show you some tricks. I won't even drink in the morning, to make sure I can do it.'

I met a lot of people like Garik in Karabagh, people who had seen indescribable things during the war, things the average person couldn't even imagine, and they relied on alcohol to keep themselves steady. You'd never see them staggering in the street or acting in the way people imagine alcoholics do. They just needed a few drinks every day to quiet the mind and keep their sanity. It seemed that a lot of money and effort had been spent on rebuilding the material casualties of the conflict, but relatively little on attempting to heal hearts and minds.

In the evening I went to Haik's house for dinner. He lived in the neighbourhood known as Hekimian 1, which apparently used to have a reputation for being a tough part of town. We talked about football along the way and how he supported Chelsea and Bayern

Munich. While his mum and sister-in-law finished cooking up a feast for us, we watched the boxing on TV. Then they started to bring out the food: countless plates of fried eggplant, peppers, salads, cheese and fruit, until we could no longer see the table. His mum sat down next to me to watch me eat. Whenever I stopped chewing, she'd ask why I wasn't eating anything. I pointed at the television, at the two men pummelling each other, and said, 'You know how in about two minutes the bell will ring and they'll stop for a break? Well, I'm having one of those breaks right now, before the next round.' She liked the analogy and piled more things on my plate in what turned into a twelve-round thriller.

After dinner Haik and I went for a stroll. It seemed everyone else was doing the same. Families and young lovers were enjoying the evening, circulating around the central part of town. 'You won't see an unmarried woman once 11 p.m. comes,' Haik said. It was considered bad form, apparently. He shared stories from his childhood, his hatred of school, his love of fishing, and how his father had died in the war. We walked to the recently built war memorial, its pale yellow stone tinged green beneath the harsh glow of the streetlamps.

Haik told me about a school friend who had been diagnosed with a fatal illness and given only two years to live. One day he saw him running home with a huge stack of videotapes. Haik asked what he was doing, and the friend said he wanted to see all the Van Damme movies before he died. Luckily it was a wrong diagnosis, and the friend went on to see many more Van Damme films.

Chapter 24

Garik Rides Again

Sayat Nova was still at the hotel and we had one last mission to undertake together. As I walked him up the main road to Garik's shop, I hoped with all my heart Garik would succeed. He had promised to ride the bike facing backwards like he had done in his youth, but I didn't know how that might pan out for someone who hadn't cycled in forty years.

Garik was waiting for me outside when I arrived, talking with a small group of friends who all gave the bike a good look up and down. He confidently took it and examined the handlebars and different specs he wasn't used to. He said he wasn't worried, and climbed on facing the back wheel. He pushed off from the pavement and began to pedal confidently. It turns out riding a bike really is something you never forget how to do, even if you do it backwards. A big smile spread across Garik's face as his friends cheered him on. I was so happy for him, an old skill and distant memory brought back to life. Relief flooded through me that he didn't fall on his face.

One of the men watching was Baris, who was going to be my driver that day to the ancient fortress of Tigranakert. He had been a driver during the war, chauffeuring generals and also carrying the wounded away from the frontline. In his taxi he swore at every other vehicle on the road and looked around nervously, always on edge.

It was Election Day and Baris showed me a pamphlet for the candidate he was voting for – Vitaly, 'a great general', according to the write-up. Baris had served under him in the army and talked about what a charismatic man he was. Within a couple of minutes, there was Vitaly himself, walking down the road with his family. Small world. Baris quickly swerved the car over and jumped out to greet him and wish him luck. Vitaly looked every inch the prospective politician: well dressed, with a head of thick, slickly combed grey hair, a pleasant smile and a commanding presence. Back in the car, Baris said he probably wouldn't win, but that both candidates were good men and he'd be happy either way. How often do you hear that during an election? I was told the same thing throughout the day by various people who all agreed both candidates were equally worthy. They didn't mind who won as long as there was peace in the region.

Tigranakert was founded in the first century BC by King Tigranes the Great, whose empire was then the strongest force east of Rome, with land that stretched from the Caspian Sea to the Mediterranean. Its armies were powerful enough to take on the Romans. This usually ended in defeat, but deserved an A for effort. The walls of the old fortress had been magnificently restored and its interior turned into a museum housing some of the artefacts found in the area – 'the pots and pans of history', as I call them. It's always the kitchen utensils that survive the most cataclysmic upheavals – a cup, or a bowl or a big decorated vase. How fancy the dinnerware was tells you how much free time a civilization had and how prominent its people were.

The distinguished-looking curator of the Tigranakert site invited me to join her for coffee. We sat in the courtyard in the shade of the trees as she explained the history of the place. She seemed very well educated and told me that the locals were trying to make her into a politician. But she was resisting. She didn't want to have meetings with horrible men all day, she said.

Baris came rushing over, saying we should go see the citadel remains nearby. He hurried me away. The citadel was very close but Baris insisted we take the car, and we sped off on the thirty-second drive. He looked on anxiously as I wandered around the excavation site where a great citadel had once stood. Within minutes, I was hustled back into the car again. I realized this was going to be the pattern for the day. Old war memories and habits weren't easily forgotten, and Baris drove his taxi like he was still in a war zone during the heat of battle.

He asked if I wanted to see the city of Aghdam, so heavily fought over during the war that it was now abandoned and in ruins. As he drove us into the city, he scanned the surroundings in every direction and said not to tell anyone he had brought me there. It was in a post-apocalyptic state with crumbling walls and not a soul in sight. A mosque stood tall in the foreground, higher than every other building. Soon it was, 'Go! Go! Go!' And without warning the tyres screeched and we roared out of town as though he was expecting a mortar attack. Pointing at the hills encircling the city, Baris gave me a full rundown of the battle positions and how the city was taken. A restored tank, gleaming like new in the sun, had been preserved as a monument, the first to be hit during the siege of Aghdam.

Back in Stepanakert, Baris said we would now be going to his house to eat and that I should take note of the route since he wouldn't be driving me back. He planned to do some drinking. He parked his taxi in a small garage and asked if I could pay him right away, so that we could finish with the business part of the day and continue as friends. His wife and daughter-in-law were busy cooking in the kitchen as his grandkids ran around the house. At last Baris looked relaxed. He unbuttoned his shirt, took a comfortable seat on the couch and in between generous servings of fish, eggplant, potatoes and vegetables downed shot after shot of vodka.

* * *

At check-out the next morning, Kristinae was wearing a beautiful purple dress and lit up the hotel reception. She smiled a lovely smile as we said our goodbyes. She thanked me for Sayat Nova and seemed sad to see me go. I was pretty sad myself. I walked over to Sayat and took a last look at my two-wheeled warrior. We didn't have much to say to each other. We had already experienced so much that no words were necessary. I knew I'd miss him, remember him always, and would feel nearly naked without him next to me as I continued through Armenia alone.

With just a light backpack now, I walked over to Garik's shop, where he was waiting for me with vodka and some fine chocolates. We drank a bit and he said some nice words and wished me a safe journey. Baris turned up, looking as rough as I did. We had both had one too many the night before. Once again I was rushed into his taxi and together we set off for the historic city of Shushi, ten kilometres away.

I read an article once about the post-war rebuilding process in Shushi and had wanted to visit ever since. It was an inspiring story in a monthly Armenian newsletter my father used to receive, about how the young people of the city had started a theatre group. Through their efforts they were trying to help reshape the attitudes of their fellow citizens coming out of the war.

Long before the war, Shushi had an illustrious history, known as a place of culture, home to writers and musicians. But during the Karabagh War, the city saw some of the toughest battles and suffered extensive damage. From the article I'd read, I expected to see quite a lot of regeneration, but was surprised how much of the city still lay in ruins. A lot of it looked dilapidated. Stepanakert had seen heavy investment, but Shushi had obviously been neglected and remained very much in a post-conflict state. The money that had come in seemed to have gone into building the large church that gleamed in the city centre. There was still a beauty about the place, though, with its quiet alleyways and ancient cobbled roads shaded by overgrown trees.

Baris drove me to the Avan Hotel. He told me to wait in the car as he raced inside to see if they had any rooms available. They did. I would miss Baris. He had opened up his home to me and protected me like I was a five-star general in his taxi.

I walked into the hotel to be greeted by yet another stunning receptionist, Lara, who just happened to be one of the loveliest creatures on God's green earth. She had a smile that made me want to spend my weekends in IKEA arguing over futons. As she checked me in and showed me to my room, I stood there covering my mouth, hoping my breath didn't smell of vodka so early in the morning.

During any long trip there's a point when loneliness comes and finds you in the most terrific burst. You don't even realize it's there, until all at once it surrounds you, haunts you and overwhelms your entire being. Your mind tells you you've isolated yourself for too long now, and it unlocks all your sublimated yearnings in a rush. As we stood among the cheap linens and new electronic fixtures in my room, I was gripped with the desire for Lara to stay there with me. I knew my fatigue and loneliness had skewed my reasoning, but I couldn't shake the thought. I just wanted to lie next to her and discuss the weather or what she watched on the telly last night. I was supremely interested in what she thought of the political situation in China at the moment. Soon, though, she was gone and I was left staring out the window at the greying clouds as her perfume lingered in the room.

Chapter 25

A Twinkle In The Cosmos

Everyone should begin their day with children bringing them flowers as they set off for work. That's how my mornings started during the three weeks I spent in the village of Mets Mantash, 100 kilometres north of Yerevan. Having completed my Tour and sent Sayat Nova to a good home, I re-joined the volunteers from the Diaspora of Armenian Culture (DAC), with whom I had done three previous campaigns.

DAC made possible my first ever visit to Armenia, all those years ago. That turned out to the best summer of my life and I continued to have a strong affection for the organization. It was founded to help the children of the poorest villages in Armenia and Karabagh. The idea was for some of us to run a summer school for the kids, full of interesting activities and sport, while the rest of the group renovated the schools.

Mets Mantash is a small village of simple crumbling homes made from cheap concrete. Its two thousand residents work the wheat fields on the outskirts of the village, tend the few cattle they have and preserve vegetables in jars to last them through the winter. There is poverty there, but they have an organized system to get through the hardship. It's a difficult life and people work hard without much expectation that things will ever change.

During the three-week summer camp, I spent my days organizing football games, teaching a little French (even though I don't speak it) and attempting to do arts and crafts that were way too complicated for the likes of me. We had about a hundred kids attending every day, energetic bundles full of shouts and screams, and we tried our best to create an interesting and eventful programme for them.

Our group was predominantly made up of French female volunteers, something the older village boys found quite enticing. I ended up spending a lot of my time at the school trying to keep these boys from interrupting our classes. It was all fairly innocent until one guy in his twenties began showing up drunk, causing mayhem. I tried being diplomatic, but I was the main male presence there and he soon became angry at me for standing in the way of his French fantasies. He'd come to the school daily and his manner became increasingly aggressive making the girls very uncomfortable. Eventually the mayor of the village had to be called to try and solve the problem. He was beyond incapable and took the boy's side. I'm not the type that gets into arguments, but I had a very Armenian shouting match with the mayor, waving my arms at him like an Italian and criticizing his disrespectful attitude towards the girls. Only afterwards did I remember that, the night before, the girls had got bored and decided to paint my nails in various pastel colours. Presumably that hadn't helped the mayor take my arguments seriously.

Somewhere in the middle of my telling the mayor that he was handling this all wrong and that I would show him why when I got drunk and visited his sister, my phone rang and it was Nayiri. Since our meeting at the Yerevan restaurant before my Tour, and my failing to gallantly accompany her home in a taxi (or steal a kiss) that night, Nayiri and I had kept in touch with phone calls and texts. While I was on the road, she'd been lecturing overseas for a few weeks. Then we met for dinner again in Yerevan after I returned from Karabagh.

Now she was on the phone and I quickly had to describe to her the scene that was taking place between the mayor and me. I told her I would call her back. We spoke that evening and she laughed hysterically at my nail polish story, meanwhile being embarrassed at the negative image of Armenia those few bad eggs in my village were giving the other volunteers. Nayiri's holidays were coming to an end and soon she would be back at the university, lecturing the new intake of students. Before she returned to work, she badly wanted to spend a few days in Georgia, at the seaside resort of Batumi, but all her friends were busy. After a day of chasing misbehaving kids, fending off a drunken vagabond and screaming at an idiot mayor, the idea of sitting on a beach sounded awfully good to me. I quickly told Nayiri I'd come with her if she could wait a week, when our time at the village would be over. She happily agreed.

* * *

Nayiri and I took the overnight bus from Yerevan to Batumi. It was a long uncomfortable ride of about 450 kilometres, with the inevitable Russian pop playing loudly through tinny speakers. The cramped space and winding roads made us both tired and I badly wanted to rest my head on Nayiri's shoulder. I could smell her floral scented hair and I desperately wanted to exchange sweet nothings with her. We spoke about how surreal it was that our friendship had continued, how one minute we were strangers in a different continent, and the next on a bus heading to Georgia's Black Sea coast together.

We grew excited as the bus approached our destination. On the outskirts it appeared like a wild rainforest. As we neared the coastline a row of low houses lined the main road – like Venice Beach in Los Angeles, except that Armenians had colonized it with barbeques, and half-naked children were running around in every direction. In the summer months this part of Georgia becomes almost like Armenia-on-sea: landlocked Armenians flock there for their holidays, the most accessible stretch of coast available to them. Nayiri promised that central Batumi would be quite different.

We spent the next few days exploring the charming old streets and boardwalks of the city. In the mornings we would have our coffee in a square that was modelled, surprisingly tastefully, on Venice's Piazza San Marco; we referred to this as 'going to Italy'. We relaxed on the quiet beaches and swam in the unexpectedly clear waters of the inaccurately named Black Sea. The beauty of our surroundings drew us closer together. We gazed into each other's eyes, lingering a little longer each time. There was a quiet understanding between us, a silent bond.

On one of our last evenings we boarded the large Ferris wheel near the shore. The lights of the city gleamed at us as we turned a splendid loop. Below us was a statue of Ali and Nino, a man and a woman made of steel slats that moved in a circle. The two shapes would turn slowly and pass through one another to make a single, unified figure. As their lips met, so did ours for the first time; without a whisper under the stars. A moment on this earth shared, a twinkle in the cosmos.

39565180R00107

Made in the USA
Charleston, SC
14 March 2015